INTERNATIONAL LEGAL RESEARCH

IN A NUTSHELL

By

MARCI B. HOFFMAN
Associate Director and
International & Foreign Law Librarian
University of California, Berkeley

ROBERT C. BERRING
Walter Perry Johnson Professor of Law
University of California, Berkeley

THOMSON

WEST

Mat #40403576

© 2008 Thomson/West
      610 Opperman Drive
      St. Paul, MN 55123
      1–800–313–9378

Printed in the United States of America

ISBN: 978–0–314–16324–0

 TEXT IS PRINTED ON 10% POST CONSUMER RECYCLED PAPER

PREFACE

This *Nutshell* is designed for the international legal research novice. We finished it at the very end of 2007—a transitional point in international legal research. Some people believe that all of international law is now available for free on the Web. Other people believe that the truth of international law lies only in the dusty volumes on a library shelf. We fall somewhere in between. Our goal is to discuss the best sources. We have focused on the print and electronic sources that are the most important, regardless of format. Most of the sources that we discuss are readily available to anyone with access to a law library or the Internet, preferably both. However, this *Nutshell* will no doubt leave some researchers wanting more or needing more in-depth research assistance. We suggest chatting with a law librarian about your specific research issue or checking out some of the books that we suggest which go into much greater detail. One such book was recently published by Marci Hoffman and Mary Rumsey, *International and Foreign Legal Research: A Coursebook* (2007).[1]

As websites change and resources evolve, we will try to keep up with these developments on our companion website, http://www.law.berkeley.edu/library/intlnutshell/. From this site, you can access

---

[1] See http://www.brill.nl/default.aspx?partid=18&pid=29350.

the websites that are cited in this *Nutshell* and learn about new stuff.

Comments and suggestions should be directed to either Bob Berring (rberring@law.berkeley.edu) or Marci Hoffman (mhoffman@law.berkeley.edu). We both read our e-mail.

ACKNOWLEDGMENTS

Bob Berring wishes to thank Meghan Corman for her help in getting the manuscript into shape. Marci Hoffman would like to express her thanks to her research assistants over the past few semesters. These brave folks include Lorrianne Carrozza, Ivan Hernandez and Eunice Koo. Marci also wishes to thank Jay Miller for . . . everything.

*

ABBREVIATIONS AND ACRONYMS

ABA	American Bar Association
ASIL	American Society of International Law
CLEA	Collection of Laws for Electronic Access
COE	Council of Europe
C.T.S.	*Consolidated Treaty Series*
EC	European Community
ECHR	European Court of Human Rights
ECJ	Court of Justice of the European Union
ECOSOC	United Nations Economic and Social Council
ECSC	European Coal and Steel Community
EEC	European Economic Community
EISIL	Electronic Information System for International Law
EU	European Union
EURATOM	European Atomic Energy Community
FAO	Food and Agriculture Organization

GATT	General Agreement on Trade and Tariffs
ICAO	International Civil Aviation Organization
ICJ	International Court of Justice
ICSID	International Center for Settlement of Investment Disputes
ICTR	International Criminal Tribunal for Rwanda
ICTY	International Criminal Tribunal for the former Yugoslavia
IGO	intergovernmental organization
ILO	International Labor Organization
IMO	International Maritime Organization
ITLOS	International Tribunal for the Law of the Sea
LII	Legal Information Institute
L.N.T.S.	*League of Nations Treaty Series*
LSN	Legal Scholarship Network
NGO	nongovernmental organization
OAS	Organization of American States
OCLC	Online Computer Library Center
ODS	Official Document System of the United Nations

OECD   Organization for Economic Co-operation and Development

OHCHR   Office of High Commissioner for Human Rights

PCA   Permanent Court of Arbitration

PCIJ   Permanent Court of International Justice

RSS   Really Simple Syndication, Rich Site Service

SSRN   Social Science Research Network

TEU   Treaty on European Union

T.I.A.S.   *Treaties and Other International Acts Series*

TIF   *Treaties in Force*

TRIPs   Agreement on Trade-Related Aspects of Intellectual Property Rights

UK   United Kingdom

U.N.   United Nations

U.N.T.S.   *United Nations Treaty Series*

UNESCO   United Nations Education, Scientific and Cultural Organization

UNHCR   United Nations High Commissioner for Refugees

UNODC   United Nations Office on Drugs and Crime

OUTLINE

OUTLINE

*

INTERNATIONAL LEGAL RESEARCH

IN A NUTSHELL

*

CHAPTER 1

INTRODUCTION AND BASIC CONCEPTS

1.1 Introduction

The study of international law is quite ancient. So long as ships have sailed the seas and nations have traded, warred and made agreements, there has been a need for international law. Because there is no governing power that stands above the nations of the world, international law has been worked out over time as a series of compromises. Thus interna-

1

tional law is much more blurry around the edges than the law of any nation.

Until recently, the practice of international law has been the province of specialists. A small, and quite often scholarly, subset of the general practice of law, these lawyers and scholars formed an identifiable community. Most law schools offered a course or two that covered some part of international law but such offerings were never part of the main curriculum.

In the past few decades, the role of international law has changed dramatically. The increasing pace of globalization has moved international law to center stage. Some law schools have integrated international or transnational features into their curriculum by adding components to the regular first-year courses, some now require a specialized course on transnational or international law, and more and more schools are offering a wide range of classes on international topics. Even a lawyer who intends to spend her life practicing law in her home state will find international issues impinging on her work. These developments combine to make the ability to carry out basic international legal research a necessary skill for every lawyer. The need for this Nutshell grows every day.

Researching international, foreign, comparative or transnational law involves a basic understanding of some key concepts before delving into the sources. Many terms employed in international, foreign and comparative research are used interchangeably and in the past have been used sloppily. Before beginning your research you will need to understand a bit of background about what you are doing. This Nutshell will focus primarily on researching international law, but there is also some coverage of foreign law. Before we begin, some basic definitions are necessary so you understand these terms as they are used throughout this Nutshell.

1.2　Basic Concepts

A.　Public International Law

Public international law governs the relationships between national governments, the relationships between intergovernmental organizations, and the relationships between national governments and intergovernmental organizations. It regulates governments and intergovernmental organizations across national boundaries. In the older world of international law, before the development of world markets and the dizzying variety of international and transnational bodies of today, public international law was the heart of the research enterprise. While it is still important, it is only the beginning.

Topics covered in public international law are varied, but the most common involve human rights, international trade, international environmental law, issues of intellectual property and much more. In the end, most of these topics will revolve around treaties as the primary body of law but they will also include the work of international organizations, both intergovernmental and nongovernmental bodies.

B. Private International Law

Private international law governs the choice of law to apply when there are conflicts in the domestic law of different countries that relate to private transactions between individual parties. In the U.S., Canada, and, most recently, England, this general area is known as *conflict of laws*. National laws are the primary sources of private international law. However, private international law is also embodied in public international law sources, especially treaties and conventions (for example, the aptly named Hague Conventions on Private International Law[1]). However, there is really no well-defined body of private international law. You will find it lurking everywhere.

Private international law deals with topics such as contracts, marriage and divorce, jurisdiction, recognition of judgments, child adoption and abduction, and many other areas.

C. Foreign Law

Foreign law is essentially the national or subnational law of a sovereign nation. It defines the role of governments with relation to the people they govern and controls relationships between people. It may regulate foreign persons and entities when they are within the borders of the national entity,

1. http://www.hcch.net/
index_en.php?act=
conventions.listing.

but it does not have effect outside the boundaries of a nation. Foreign law is embodied in constitutions, statutes, regulations, and court decisions. Constitutions, statutes, and regulations are primary sources of law for all jurisdictions. Court decisions are also primary sources of law in common law jurisdictions, but are considered secondary sources of law in civil law jurisdictions. If you need to know the law in France on a certain topic (and you are not French), then it is a matter of consulting foreign law.

There are currently five legal systems in the world today: civil law, common law, customary law, religious law, and mixed legal systems. Until recently, one would have listed communist law as a separate system but with Vietnam and China looking and more and more like mixed systems based in civil law, only North Korea can claim a truly communist ideology and its legal system is sui generic. Many systems are mixed because two or more legal systems are applied within the jurisdiction.

For a quick look at the major legal systems (civil law, common law, etc.), see World Legal Systems.[2] It provides good background, it is on the internet and it is free. What could be better?

D. Comparative Law

Comparative law is "the study of the similarities and differences between the laws of two or more

2.   http://www.droitcivil. uottawa.ca/world-legal- systems/eng-monde.phh.

countries, or between two or more legal systems. Comparative law is not itself a system of law or a body of rules, but rather a method or approach to legal inquiry."[3]

Since comparative law is not a body of law itself but instead consists of comparing existing systems, the most useful sources are books and articles that focus on the comparison of national law or legal systems. Comparative law is largely the turf of scholars and academics and it seldom has an application in the practice of law. It is mysterious to many American legal researchers because it often calls for the mastery of more than one language, and mastery at a very sophisticated level. However, Professor Alan Watson has said "[c]omparative law provides unique insights into law in general, the forces behind legal change, law and society."[4] For more background information, see Peter de Cruz, *Comparative Law in a Changing World* (3rd ed. 2005), Mary Ann Glendon, *Comparative Legal Traditions in a Changing World* (2nd ed. 1999) and Alan Watson, *Comparative Law: Law, Reality and Society* (2007).

E. Transnational Law

Transnational law generally includes "all law which regulates actions or events that transcend national frontiers. Both public and private interna-

3. Robert C. Berring et al., *How to Find the Law* 565 (9th ed. 1989).

4. Alan Watson, *Comparative Law: Law, Reality and Society*, see Preface (2007).

tional law are included, as are other rules which do not wholly fit into such standard categories."[5] Works on this subject invariably focus on the legal relationship between a person and alien individuals or corporations, most frequently in commercial, industrial or investment situations.[6] Transnational law has been the locus of much of the growth in international practice. It is a field that is defining itself as the world shrinks due to globalization.

Transnational law is another term that is hard to pin down. When you encounter it, it will most likely lead to one of the other sources. Remember, these are areas of research that lack hard and fast boundaries.

F. Soft Law

Soft law encompasses non-binding documents or instruments (such as guidelines, declarations, and principles) that may have use politically, but are not enforceable. Not that any international law is really enforceable, but soft law does not even have the pretense of being more than aspirational. Soft law has been effective in international economic law and international environmental law and is often created by international organizations.

Some examples of soft law include "Norms on the Responsibilities of Transnational Corporations and Other Business Enterprises with Regard to Human

5. Philip C. Jessup, *Transnational Law* 2 (1956).

6. *Parry and Grant Encyclopaedic Dictionary of Inter-* *national Law* 511 (2nd ed. 2003).

Rights" or the FAO's Code of Conduct for Responsible Fisheries (1995). For more information on soft law, see Dinah Shelton, *Soft Law*.[7]

G. Supranational Law

Practically speaking, there is only one supranational legal order—the European Union (EU). A supranational organization has the following characteristics: (1) it has powers that its member states do not have because they surrendered those powers to it; (2) it may enact rules that preempt the laws and regulations of its member states; and (3) it can grant rights and privileges to the nationals of its member states, which those nationals may directly invoke.

The EU is a highly articulated and complex organization that will enter into our discussions at many points. The various components of the EU generate many terms and concepts that will be used throughout this book. By no means do we hope to cover all the terminology encountered when doing research in this area. Indeed much of the study of international and foreign legal systems is laden with unfamiliar terms. To alleviate this problem we will outline some background sources in Chapter 2. But this is a Nutshell so it will use a very broad brush to paint a very complicated picture.

7. Dinah L. Shelton, "Soft Law", *Handbook of International Law* (2008), available at SSRN: http://ssrn.com/abstract=1003387.

1.3 Sources of Law

One of the keys to understanding international and foreign legal materials is recognizing that there is no single source of authority to which you can turn. Describing the sources of law in a single legal system is much more straightforward than trying to do the same for all other systems, to say nothing of the world of international law. Because each nation is its own sovereign entity, it possesses primary and secondary sources of law. This means that some sources have binding authority, some are considered persuasive, and others are used to locate binding and persuasive authority. Even more important, each nation has the power to enforce its laws. If it is to remain sovereign, it must have control of its people and its territory, and its laws must be binding. Such national law is embodied in constitutions, statutes, regulations, and court decisions. Constitutions, statutes, and regulations are primary sources of law for all jurisdictions. Court decisions are also primary sources of law in common law jurisdictions, but are considered secondary sources of law in civil law jurisdictions. In later chapters we will show you how to get a basic grasp of how the system of each nation works. You will find that lots of help awaits you.

Customary law plays a role in some legal systems, though no country operates solely under a customary law system. Customary law tends to govern areas of personal conduct, inheritance, and marriage. Most often, customary law is unwritten, and is dispensed by persons with elected or hereditary roles within a community. If this sounds strange to you, think of the common law that undergirds the judicial opinions of American and English courts.

The sources of public international law lack sovereign power. There is no central authority and no ability to make public international law stick. It is true that the nations can combine to punish a rogue nation or to enforce a norm, but these are ad hoc occurrences and not part of a system. Sometimes nations combine as rogues to violate established norms. The world is far from simple. Thus the sources of public international law are always subject to dispute and interpretation. This does not mean that they are not important, but it does mean that they must be viewed in context.

The traditional sources of public international law are listed below. Their authority is based on Article 38 of the International Court of Justice Statute (the ICJ Statute) which is "generally considered to be the most authoritative enumeration of the sources of international law."[8]

- International conventions (treaties);
- Customary law (general practice of States and intergovernmental organizations that are legally binding and generally recognized by all States);
- General principles of law; and
- Judicial decisions and the teachings of the most highly qualified publicists of the various nations.

8. Thomas Buergenthal & Sean D. Murphy, *Public Inter-* *national Law in a Nutshell* 19 (4th ed. 2007).

To provide you with a ground level view of how the different legal systems use authority we refer you to the chart set out below.

	Common Law	Civil Law	Public International Law	Private International Law
Primary Sources	Constitutions	Constitutions	Treaties	National Law
	Statutes/Codes	Statutes/Codes	Customary Law	Treaties
	Regulations	Regulations	Generally Recognized Principles of Law	Customary Law
	Court Decisions			
Secondary Sources	Scholarly Commentary	Court Decisions	Court Decisions	Court Decisions
		Scholarly Commentary	Teachings of Publicists (Scholarly Commentary)	Scholarly Commentary

1.4   Types of Legal Sources

Researching international and foreign law requires that you look at a variety of sources for law and for commentary. You will encounter tools that are not familiar parts of the usual American legal research problem. The sources of law and secondary materials will be available in many different print and electronic sources. Though some may look quite different than what you are accustomed to using, there are more similarities than differences. Throughout this Nutshell, you will learn about many types of legal materials, including books, documents, commercial databases, freely available websites, journal articles, and people. Research in international law is becoming more straight-forward every day. This is a good thing because if you are a law student or young lawyer reading this chapter, international legal questions will find you.

CHAPTER 2

SOME BASICS AS YOU BEGIN

2.1 Introduction

If you are new to international law research, you will not get very far before you encounter something confusing. Many terms, phrases, and abbreviations that are used in international law are unfamiliar to the typical U.S. researcher. The good news is that just as with the abbreviations that appear in American legal materials, you do not have to memorize the meaning of every one of them. The skill you need is the ability to look up what an abbreviation means. The following sources may be useful for finding definitions and for deciphering the alphabet soup of international organizations and materials. You will find these sources that we describe at the

Reference Desk of most large libraries, and, where noted, online.

2.2 Abbreviations

Some of the standard tools useful for deciphering American legal abbreviations can also prove useful for international legal abbreviations. One such tool is *Bieber's Dictionary of Legal Abbreviations* (Prince ed., 5th ed. 2001); the earlier edition is also available on LexisNexis. This source, often just called "Bieber" by experienced researchers, is a goldmine. It is the tool that the professionals use first, so you should use it, too.

A few abbreviation guides are geared towards citations specific to international and foreign law. One good guide is Igor I. Kavass, *World Dictionary of Legal Abbreviations* (1991–). This multivolume set is arranged by language and by subject. For special help when it comes to understanding citations to case reporters from other jurisdictions and from international courts, see *Noble's International Guide to the Law Reports* (2002). Although Donald Raistrick, *Index to Legal Citations and Abbreviations* (2nd ed. 1993), is a bit dated, it is helpful when working with European abbreviations. One of the more pleasant features of abbreviations is that they usually stay the same over time, so that even a dated source can be of help.

The most comprehensive website for abbreviations is the Cardiff Index to Legal Abbreviations.[1]

1. http://www.legalabbrevs.cardiff.ac.uk/.

This index focuses on abbreviations from English language legal publications from the British Isles, the Commonwealth and the United States. It includes abbreviations covering international and comparative law sources. This site is simple to use and it is free. Set out below are some screen shots for the website with an example of how to use it. If you remain a fan of books, a guide for abbreviations by foreign jurisdiction is the *Guide to Foreign and International Legal Citations* (2006)—luckily, it's available on the web too.[2]

2. http://law.nyu.edu/journals/jilp/gfilc.html.

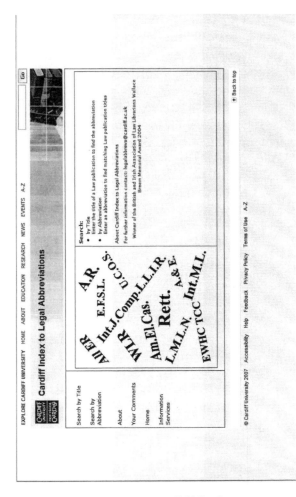

Figure 1: Cardiff Index

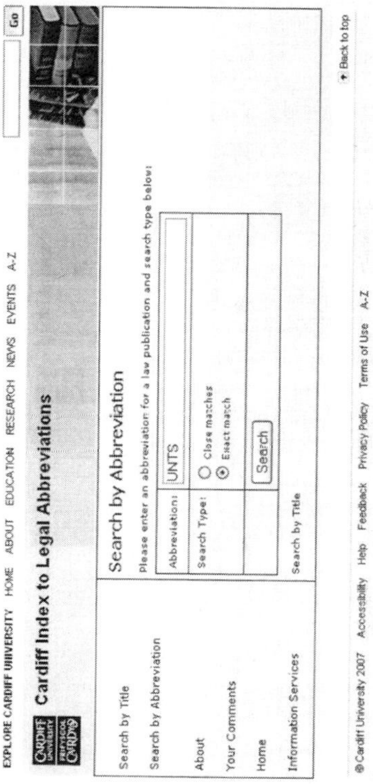

Figure 2: Search Screen

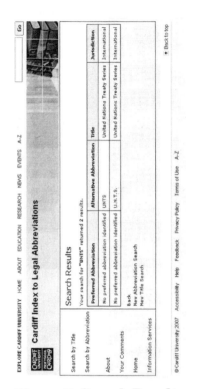

Figure 3: Search Results

2.3 Dictionaries and Encyclopedias

Dictionaries and encyclopedias help the researcher locate definitions and general descriptions of international and foreign legal terms and concepts. They can provide the context and background that are necessary when one is working in an unfamiliar area. Remember that knowing the terrain is vital.

Even elementary background sources can be a huge help. The very best source for information on international law is the *Encyclopedia of Public International Law* (1981–1990, 1992–). This set provides a fairly complete analysis of many public international law concepts and subjects. It is readable and straightforward and can be a real lifesaver. Other useful, yet less extensive works, include *Parry & Grant Encyclopaedic Dictionary of International Law* (2nd ed. 2004) and Edmund Jan Osmanczyk, *The Encyclopedia of the United Nations and International Agreements* (3rd ed. 2003). The latter two sources are commonly found in academic law libraries.

There are two additional dictionaries that can offer basic help. They are James R. Fox, *Dictionary of International and Comparative Law* (3rd ed. 2003) and Boleslaw A. Boczek, *International Law: A Dictionary* (2005).

While there are many web-based dictionaries, there are few reliable and authoritative legal dictionaries to be found in cyberspace and really nothing that focuses on international law. This will likely change, but for now, to quote the great wise man, it is what it is. Try a book.

Help with context, definitions and basic explanations can be found in the *Restatement of the Law, Third, the Foreign Relations Law of the United States* (1987, annual supplements).[3] Like other elements in the Restatement series, these volumes

3. Also available on Lexis-Nexis and Westlaw.

provide a comprehensible structure with excellent content and a plethora of cross-references. This is a good source for getting an understanding of the basic doctrines of international law from a U.S. perspective. The Restatements are produced under the auspices of the American Law Institute and reflect the best thinking of American lawyers, judges and academics. It is a powerful persuasive source that works hard to explain itself.

2.4   Research Guides

One of the most important tenets of carrying out efficient legal research is to find someone who has done the work for you. No matter what the research problem one encounters, it is likely that someone has worked on it before. The community of people who work in the area of international legal research have a true egalitarian spirit, and many have tried to leave a map for those who follow. For example, many international law librarians and lawyers create research guides that focus on a particular topic or jurisdiction. By using these guides, the novice (and sometimes even the expert) researcher can locate both print and electronic sources quickly and efficiently.

A magnificent source that is available via the internet is the American Society of International Law's Guide to Electronic Sources for International Law.[4] The Guide is one of the most highly acclaimed research guides on international law. It

4.   http://www.asil.org/ resource/home.htm.

contains eleven chapters and covers a variety of topics: treaties, commercial arbitration law, economic law, the human rights, and more. This is a great place to start.

Two other important collections of research guides cover a variety of international law topics and foreign jurisdictions: LLRX.com[5] and Globalex.[6] Globalex contains guides prepared by law librarians from around the world. Some are done from the perspective of academic law librarians; some are focused on questions closer to the practice of law. The researcher who finds a guide at LLRX or Globalex has a leg up on any research problem. Other useful guides include:

Claire Germain, *Germain's Transnational Law Research* (1991–), this looseleaf publication focuses on selected topics and provides guides for a few European countries. The chapter on French law is available on the web.[7]

Guide to International Legal Research (2002–) provides a solid basis from which to start research for both international legal topics and selected foreign legal jurisdictions.

The International Lawyer's Deskbook (2nd ed. 2003), a basic guide to information on selected topics that are of particular interest to the American lawyer.

5. http://www.llrx.com/ category/1050.

6. http://www. nyulawglobal.org/globalex/ index.html.

7. http://library2.lawschool. cornell.edu/encyclopedia/ countries/france/default.htm.

Foreign Law Guide[8] covers many jurisdictions and is the best source for locating foreign law. You will hear much more about this resource elsewhere in the Nutshell.

2.5 Directories

Most intergovernmental organizations and non-governmental organizations have websites. These sites provide information about the organizations and usually contain documents and reports created by the various bodies. As with everything else on the internet, the quality depends on the source who produces the website. Often, a Google search using the name of the organization will yield a link to the relevant website, or use the acronym for the organization. In the event you need a more organized approach, these web directories can be useful. Note that they are assembled for free by librarians who are just trying to help. This is part of that community of researchers which we discussed earlier.

- International Agencies and Information on the Web (University of Michigan)[9]

8. http://www.foreign lawguide.com/ (subscription database). The print version is called Thomas H. Reynolds & Arturo A. Flores, *Foreign Law: Current Sources of Codes and Basic Legislation in Jurisdictions of the World* (1989–). At some point in the near future, the print will be discontinued in favor of the electronic version.

9. http://www.lib.umich. edu/govdocs/intl.html.

- International Organizations Website (North-western University)[10]

Print directories should not be ignored (really) since they can provide descriptive information on a wide range of organizations, particularly by subject or geographic region. The best include *Encyclopedia of Associations: International Organizations* (1989–); *The Europa Directory of International Organizations* (1999–); and *Yearbook of International Organizations* (1967–).[11]

2.6 Classics

International law has been around for centuries. Because of this long history and because of the fact that international legal norms cross boundaries and lack a central authority, the writings of great scholars take on an importance that goes beyond anything that exists in the American system. The closest analogy would be the influence on federal civil procedure exerted by *Wright and Miller on Federal Courts*, but even that is based on interpreting underlying legislation. When it comes to the influential works on international law, there is a special kind of personal authority. Of course the original author of the work may be long gone, but the prestige carries on. The researcher can use these works for background, for research guidance or to construct persuasive arguments.

10. http://www.library.northwestern.edu/govinfo/resource/internat/igo.html.

11. All of these are available electronically by subscription; check with a librarian.

There are many classic works in international law and these are good places for the novice to get familiar with the framework of this topic. Some of the most highly regarded include Ian Brownlie, *Principles of Public International Law* (6th ed. 2003); L. Oppenheim, *Oppenheim's International Law* (Robert Jennings & Arthur Watts, eds., 9th ed. 1992); Peter Malanczuk, *Akehurst's Modern Introduction to International Law* (8th rev. ed. 2002); and Malcolm Shaw, *International Law* (5th ed. 2003). While there is no comprehensive list of these classic works, the following sources list many of these titles: International Legal Research Tutorial: Essential Sources,[12] Researching Public International Law: Treatises,[13] and HeinOnline's Legal Classics: International Law.[14]

If you are unsure, ask your professor or a librarian about what is considered a classic in the field in which you are working.

12. http://www.law.duke.edu/ilrt/sources_5.htm.

13. http://www.law.columbia.edu/library/Research_Guides/internat_law/pubint#Treatises.

14. http://heinonline.org/HOL/Index?index=beal/sub15 & collection=beal.

CHAPTER 3

FOREIGN AND COMPARATIVE LAW

3.1 Introduction

The focus of the Nutshell is researching international law. While international law is distinct from foreign and comparative law, we recognize that those doing international legal research often end up doing some foreign legal research as well. While research in comparative law is a much more limited endeavor, being mostly the province of academic writers, it makes sense to treat it in this book as well. Therefore we will address researching foreign and comparative law in this chapter. The field of foreign law is a vast one so be forewarned that we

25

will not go into great detail for any specific country. Our goal will be to provide some basic strategies for locating and researching the domestic law of another country—also known as foreign law—with a bit of comparative law research advice in the section that follows.

For the purposes of this chapter, "foreign law" is the national (also referred to as domestic or internal) law of any country, other than the United States. (Assuming that you are a researcher in the United States, if you are from another country, substitute its name). Comparative law is "the study of the similarities and differences between the laws of two or more countries, or between two or more legal systems. Comparative law is not itself a system of law or a body of rules, but rather a method or approach to legal inquiry."[1]

While research methods will vary depending on the country you are researching, when beginning to research a legal system, it's a good idea to get a basic understanding of the structure of the legal system. There are several ways to do this. First, determine if the country in question is a civil law system based upon codes that draw upon a Roman law heritage, a common law system (such as the United States) that springs from English tradition, or a mixed system. Some legal systems are also influenced by religious law or by custom. A quick way to determine the type of system for the country

1. Robert C. Berring et al., *How to Find the Law* 565 (9th ed. 1989).

in question is to consult the free website, World Legal System (see Figure 1).[2] For more information on legal systems generally, see H. Patrick Glen, *Legal Traditions of the World* (3rd ed. 2007).

Next, look for a source that explains the legal system of the country that you are researching. This is especially important if you do not have much background in the national system that you are approaching. Luckily there are some quite reliable sources for getting rich background information. Perhaps the most widely used and respected source is *Foreign Law Guide*.[3] This source will give you background on the country, its legal system, its legal publications and, best of all, sources of English translations of its materials. An expert in the country you are looking up could probably find mistakes in the description, no surprise since this set is covering so much ground, but it is generally reliable and, as noted, everyone uses it. See also *Modern Legal Systems Cyclopedia* (1984–) or *Introduction to Foreign Legal Systems* (1994). You should also see if a specific overview or a research guide is available for your country since these sources usually provide an outline of the legal structure. Some ideas on how to find these resources will be covered later in this chapter.

2. http://www.droitcivil.uottawa.ca/world-legal-systems/eng-monde.php.

3. Thomas H. Reynolds & Arturo A. Flores, *Foreign Law: Current Sources of Codes and Basic Legislation in Jurisdictions of the World* (1989–). The print will be discontinued in favor of the electronic version, Foreign Law Guide, http://www.foreignlawguide.com/ (subscription database).

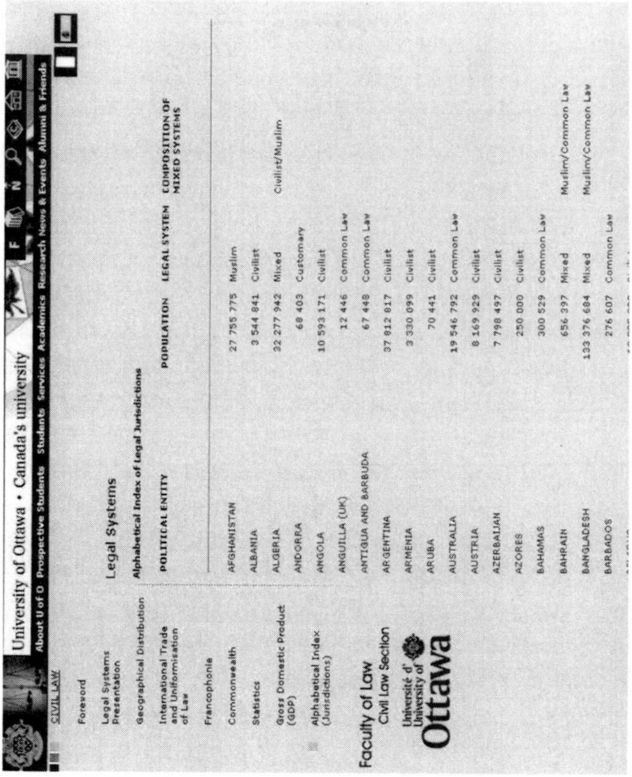

Figure 1: World Legal Systems Website

3.2   Civil Law Versus Common Law

Before jumping into foreign legal research, you should understand some fundamentals of civil and common law. Civil law refers to a legal tradition based on Roman law and codified in the *Corpus*

Juris Civilis of Justinian. This tradition that initially developed in Continental Europe eventually developed into codified Roman law and uncodified Roman law. A key feature of civil law is its system and structure, often relying on declarations of broad, general principles.

The Common law legal tradition evolved in England beginning in the 11th century. Disputes that have been adjudicated comprise the set of principles that courts, usually courts of appeal, produce as judgments. Common law is the foundation of private law for England, Wales and Ireland, forty-nine U.S. states, as well as most countries that received that law as colonies of the British Empire.

Below are some basic comparisons between the two basic systems. These are quite simplistic, but they do represent some fundamental differences.

CIVIL LAW JURISDICTIONS	COMMON LAW JURISDICTIONS
Relies primarily on legislation to develop and enact laws.	Relies primarily on court decisions to interpret legislation as well as develop law
Historical Concept: A single, complete, coherent, and logical system to govern all legal relationships was possible to develop and follow.	Historical Concept: Legislation (by the ruling authority) was considered as a suspension of the "common law" that governed the everyday affairs of men; thus, people were suspicious of how legislation was to be applied.
Favors predictability and stability, but is generally very inflexible because it can be changed only by legislative action.	Favors flexibility, although predictability comes from the principle of *stare decisis* (do not disturb a settled point).
Civil law attorneys tend to interpret the law expansively in order to add the flexibility necessary to apply the legislation to new situations when they arise. However,	While common law attorneys tend to interpret legislative law narrowly, common law courts tend to interpret legislation more broadly than civil law courts, and this pro-

CIVIL LAW JURISDICTIONS	COMMON LAW JURISDICTIONS
the current trend in some civil law jurisdictions is for lawyers to keep informed about (and often use) prior judicial decisions in new cases.	vides the flexibility to address new situations without new legislative action.
Trial judge has the responsibility to "find the truth." Thus, the judge (court) often identifies the legal issue(s), investigates the facts, selects and questions the witnesses, and assumes the procedural initiative.	Relies on the "adversary system"; thus, the court is "passive." The court solves only those issues that are put before it; the attorneys identify and frame the issues and then are the advocates for their respective sides. "Truth" is ultimately found by the court, with help from the jury, through the passive decision making that separates persuasive arguments and evidence from unpersuasive ones.
Relies primarily on deductive reasoning.	Relies on a combination of inductive, deductive, and analogical reasoning.

Table 1: Civil versus Common Law Jurisdictions[4]

In a civil law system, primary sources include: constitutions, statutes/codes, and regulations. Secondary sources include: court decisions (jurisprudence) and scholarly commentary. In a common law system, primary sources include all of the above plus judicial decisions. The commentary of scholars is considered to be a secondary source. The rule of thumb is that in civil law countries the code is

4. This table is reproduced from: http://www.uni-trier.de/uni/fb5/ffa/kursunterlagen/SS 07daspit/legalwriting/Lecture1/ BASICPRINCIPLES.doc.   At the time of printing of this Nutshell, this site is no longer available. This is an example of one of the problems with the web.

paramount and decisions of the court are just interpretations of it. In common law countries judicial decisions are statements of the law itself. Of course, this is an extreme simplification, but it is a basis from which to build. Most commentators feel that the two systems are moving closer to one another as time passes. For more information on civil and common law, see John G. Apple and Robert P. Deyling, *A Primer on the Civil–Law System*.[5]

3.3 Types of Sources

Constitutions are widely available both in the original language and in English. Several websites are available to access these primary documents, see for example the University of Richmond's Constitution Finder[6] and the International Constitutional Law Project.[7] These are good sources and they are free. Another widely available source is *Constitutions of the Countries of the World* (1971–), available in print and electronically by subscription.[8]

Statutory law is prevalent in both kinds of legal systems and is published in several types of sources:

5. http://www.fjc.gov/public/pdf.nsf/lookup/CivilLaw.pdf/$file/CivilLaw.pdf.

6. http://confinder.richmond.edu/.

7. http://www.servat.unibe.ch/law/icl/index.html.

8. Each chapter provides some historical information, and the older versions help the researcher track changes to the language. Also available on the web at http://www.oceanalaw.com, by subscription.

- Official or national gazettes (usually released daily by national governments, these may contain laws, notices, and other information; see Government Gazettes Online[9]).

- Session laws (laws published chronologically, in print or electronic form).

- Codified Laws (a subject arrangement of laws).

- Subject compilations, other than codes.

9. Provides access to many country gazettes and information on the web, http://www. lib.umich.edu/govdocs/gazettes/index.htm.

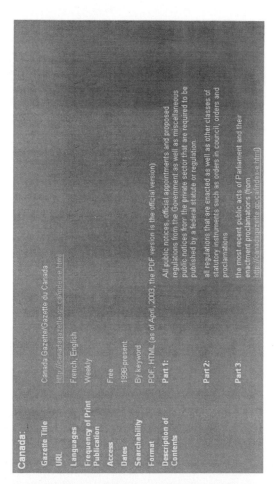

Figure 2: Information on the Canada Gazette from the Michigan website

Figure 3: Canada Gazette[10]

10. Part III: Acts of Parliament, http://canadagazette.gc.ca/partIII/index-e.html.

Court decisions are also available from a variety of sources:

- Official reporters (publications deemed as the primary and official source of case law).

- Commercial or unofficial source (most websites would be considered unofficial, unless it's the Court's site; for example, see the High Court of Australia decisions available on the AustLII website[11]).

- Journals (used a great deal in some jurisdictions, like Germany and France).

- Topic specific compilations.

11. AustLII, http://www.austlii.edu.au/au/cases/cth/HCA/. While the site says the "[t]his database contains all officially reported and selected unreported decisions of the High Court of Australia," there is no indication that the cases available on AustLII are official.

[Home] [Databases] [WorldLII] [Search] [Feedback]

High Court of Australia

You are here: AustLII >> Databases >> High Court of Australia >> 2007 >> [2007] HCA 1

[Database Search] [Name Search] [Recent Decisions] [Noteup] [Download] [Help]

Sons of Gwalia Ltd v Margaretic [2007] HCA 1; (2007) 232 ALR 232; (2007) 81 ALJR 525 (31 January 2007)

Last Updated: 31 January 2007

HIGH COURT OF AUSTRALIA

GLEESON CJ,

GUMMOW, KIRBY, HAYNE, CALLINAN, HEYDON AND CRENNAN JJ

Matter No S208/2006

SONS OF GWALIA LTD (SUBJECT TO DEED

OF COMPANY ARRANGEMENT) APPELLANT

AND

LUKA MARGARETIC & ANOR RESPONDENTS

Figure 4: Unofficial Case from AustLII Website

3.4   Developing a Research Strategy

Once you understand the nature of the legal system in question, you should determine exactly what you need. Do you need a constitution, a specific statute, a case, or general information about a country's legal system? Do you have a citation to the law or to an article? What are the dates? Do you need the complete text of the law, a summary, an English translation, or a detailed explanation? Will an electronic version be sufficient or do you need an official print source? Here are some tips to help answer these many questions:

- Use a secondary source to start your research. These sources describe the law or legal issue, provide commentary, and put the issue into context.

- Identify the sources of law for the country. Does the country publish codes, compilations of statutes, or reporters? A good source for gathering this information is *Foreign Law Guide* (noted above).

- Once you have identified the source, consult a library catalog or other bibliographic database to determine if the item is available.

As noted above, using a research guide or an introductory source is a good place to begin researching the law or legal system of another country. Most of these kinds of tools will outline the structure of the legal system and the sources of law that are available. Research guides and introductions may be contained in journal articles or in a chapter of a more general book.

We have already mentioned the grand-daddy of all such sources: T. Reynolds & A. Flores, *Foreign Law: Current Sources of Codes and Basic Legislation in Jurisdictions of the World* (1989–). The electronic version of this source is *Foreign Law Guide*.[12] The print version will cease publication sometime in 2008, so the electronic version will be all that will be updated after that date. This source is one of the best to consult when researching foreign law. It contains information on nearly 200 jurisdictions and each country section contains the following information: a brief history of the legal system (including references to other introductory sources); an outline of the major publications (including major codifications, official gazettes, compilations or official codifications, session laws, court reports, and internet resources); and a section of laws organized by subject headings. While this source does not cover every country nor every law within a country, it does contain a lot of information and is always worth consulting.

12. http://www.foreign lawguide.com, a subscription service. At some point soon, the print version of this source, will be discontinued.

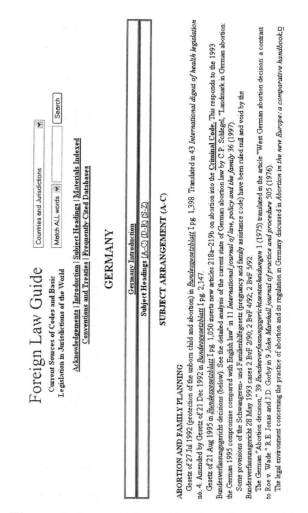

Figure 5: Sample from *Foreign Law Guide*

While there is no other source which covers as many countries as the *Foreign Law Guide*, there are a few other basic sources to consult at the start of any research projects. See Claire Germain, *Germain's Transnational Law Research* (1991–).[13] The focus of this loose-leaf set is the countries of Europe. The chapters are arranged by subject. You might also check the *Guide to International Legal Research* (2002–). The final resource to consider is *Modern Legal Systems Cyclopedia* (K. Redden ed., 1984–) which covers 10 regions, but the information and frequency of updates in this set varies from chapter to chapter. As ever, consult a librarian about what sources are available in your library.

Legal researchers are fortunate that the web has proven a useful vehicle for accessing country research guides. While these guides are available on a growing number of different websites, there are a few sites that should be checked first since they provide links to other sites. These sites include:

- An Annotated Guide to Web Sites around the World (produced by the staff of the Harvard Law Library)[14] covers regional and national law sites.

- A Selective List of Guides to Foreign Legal Research (compiled by the staff at Columbia Law Library).[15]

13. The chapter on France is available on the web at http://www.lawschool.cornell.edu/library/encyclopedia/countries/france/default.htm.

14. http://www.law.harvard.edu/library/services/research/guides/international/web_resources/.

15. http://www.law.columbia.edu/library/Research_Guides/foreign_law/foreignguide.

- Globalex[16]

- LLRX.com Country Guides.[17]

- Guide to Law Online (Library of Congress).[18]

- World Law Legal Information Institute.[19]

While you can access many research guides and a lot of information over the web, some of the best introductions to the law of a country are in print sources. For example, William E. Butler, *Russian Law* (2nd ed. 2003), Nigel Foster, *German Legal System & Laws* (3rd ed. 2002), and *Introduction to Turkish Law* (Tugrul Ansay & Don Wallace, Jr. eds., 5th ed. 2005). Other useful sources available in many academic and law firm libraries include the *Doing Business In . . .* books. For example, *Doing Business in Mexico* (1980–), *Doing Business in Argentina* (1998–), or *Doing Business in Asia* (1991–). Some of these print sources are available on Lexis-Nexis too. Also consider sources that focus on the geographic region when looking for laws or information on a specific legal system. Sources on the region may contain sections or chapters on the country in question. See *BNA's Eastern Europe Reporter (1991–)*, *Taxation in Latin America* (1987–), or *International Commercial Arbitration in Asia* (2006–).

16. http://www. nyulawglobal.org/globalex/.

17. http://www.llrx.com/ category/1050.

18. http://www.loc.gov/law/ help/guide.html.

19. http://www.worldlii. org/.

Many of the sources for abbreviations are listed in Chapter 2 of this Nutshell. Some abbreviations can be located in the source itself or you may need a guide that focuses on a single jurisdiction, like, Jorge A. Vargas, *Mexican Legal Dictionary and Desk Reference* (2003). A very handy guide is available from New York University Law School, *Guide to Foreign and International Legal Citations* (2006).[20] This tool provides information on available legal sources and how to abbreviate and cite them.

3.5   Looking for Foreign Law

There are generally two approaches for looking for foreign law—by subject or by jurisdiction. If you are looking for a specific piece of legislation, the tools mentioned above are very useful. *Foreign Law Guide* is particularly useful for this purpose since it contains a listing of selected laws arranged by subject for each country. Country research guides may not provide guidance for all specific laws, but they will provide information on compilations of laws or specific codes. Be sure to look for subject compilations; for example, laws on investment are contained in a set called *Investment Laws of the World* (1972–). As mentioned above, also consider sources from the region where the country is located.

The ABA publishes a book that is quite useful for the practicing lawyer, called *International Lawyer's Deskbook* (Lucinda A. Low et al., eds., 2nd ed.

20.   http://www.law.nyu. edu/journals/jilp/gfilc.html.

2002). It provides context and citations to laws and secondary sources on a variety of topics, such as arbitration, international litigation, child adoption, and more.

Another source that is available in most law libraries is the *Martindale Hubbell International Law Digest* (1993–2006).[21] While the country coverage is limited, it is a worthwhile place to start since it does provide an outline of major laws by topic.

A more extensive source is *International Encyclopaedia of Laws* (dates vary). Arranged by topic (civil procedure, contracts, environmental law, family and succession, social security, etc.), it covers many jurisdictions and provides more information than either of the above-mentioned sources.

Look for subject compilations, digests, and periodicals that cover your topic. Subject compilations such as *Tax Laws of the World* (dates vary), *Commercial Laws of the World* (dates vary), *Digest of Commercial Laws of the World* (1998–) and *Commercial Laws of Europe* (1978–) can be of great help. You will note that they tend to treat topics that generate transactions and business. *Foreign Law Guide* provides a good listing of subject compilations under the section called "Materials Indexed."

Secondary legislation, regulations and administrative decisions are often sought after and are even more elusive than statutory law and case law. Start

21. Available on LexisNexis. The print was discontinued and now the only other access is on CD–ROM.

by using the sources mentioned in the above sections. Secondary sources may be another way to track down relevant sources. If a country publishes an official gazette (as most civil law systems do), you have a better chance of locating regulations, notices, circulars, etc. See Government Gazettes Online[22] or *Foreign Law Guide* for more information.

3.6   Translated Material

Most U.S. lawyers and law students want foreign laws to appear in English, even if they have the requisite language abilities. There are many sources that have English language translations, some available by country, by region, or by topic. Be aware of the limitations of translations:

- Translations, even if done under the auspices of a government agency, are not necessarily official or authoritative. The only exceptions are jurisdictions where English is one of the official languages.

- Translations can be inaccurate. Many legal terms and phrases do not mean the same thing in every language or every legal system. Think of the problems of jargon and word usage encountered by students in law school, add in a different language and perhaps a different legal structure, and the problem becomes apparent.

22. Provides access to many country gazettes and information on the web, http:// www.lib.umich.edu/govdocs/ gazettes/index.htm.

Be sure the translation was done by someone with knowledge of the country's legal system.

- Translations may not include the most current revisions of the law.

- Some topics have more translations than other topics; areas such as business, trade, taxation, and commercial law tend to have more English language sources than areas dealing with family law or social issues.

Translations can be found in a variety of sources: books, journals, loose-leaf sets, websites (both available free of charge and in fee-based databases). There are many English language compilations, especially in the areas of taxation, trade commercial and business law. Other areas of law may not have readily available English language translations. Another thing to consider is the date of the translation. Be sure to read the translated version carefully because some compilations may contain only an abstract of the law or an explanation and not the full text of the law.

Loose-leaf services (sources that are frequently updated) and journals can be a fruitful sources for English translations. As mentioned earlier, the section called "Materials Indexed" in *Foreign Law Guide* is a good listing to check. Also, see Sources of International and Foreign Law in English for another listing of translations by topic.[23] Neither of

23. http://www.law.uiuc.
edu/library/ref_sources_intl_
foreignlaw_english.asp.

these sources is complete, but they provide good starting places.

There are also some good websites for accessing reliable translations. Many of these websites are created by international organizations. Some of these include WIPO's Collection of Laws for Electronic Access (CLEA),[24] the ILO's NATLEX database,[25] and the Migration Law Database produced by the International Organization for Migration.[26] See Appendix C for a list of more websites containing translated national laws.

24. http://www.wipo.int/ clea/en/index.jsp.

25. http://www.ilo.org/dyn/ natlex/natlex_browse.home.

26. http://www.imldb.iom. int/.

Brazil	Copyright (Software), Law, 19-02-1998, No. 9.609(br001)
Law No. 9.609, of February 19, 1998 which regulates the protection of "software"	
Text was notified to WTO on January 26, 2000 in English. Listing is available. Main dedicated text.	
Subject matters	Copyright and Related Rights Civil judicial procedures and remedies Criminal procedures
Date of basic text	February 19, 1998
Date of entry into force of basic text	June 19, 1998
Officially published in	"Diário Oficial", 20/02/1998, No. 36, Seção 1
Note	Notification States: "Article 14, caput, paragraphs 1 and 5, which contains provisions concerning civil actions related to the violation of software copyright; and paragraphs 2, 3 and 4, which contain provisions concerning "in camera proceedings" and provisional remedies related to software copyright." "Articles 12 and 13, which contain provisions concerning criminal actions and violations related to software copyright."
Relations with other texts	BR_1 is referred to in Copyright, Decree, 20/04/1998, No. 2.556 BR_7
Text is available	in English. On-line fulltext (html)(pdf) 8 pages Note:WTO Ducument IP/N/1/BRA/C/1 in Portuguese Text available only in paper format. in Portuguese Text available only in paper format. in Portuguese Text available only in paper format.
Title in French	Loi n° 9.609, du 19 février 1998 qui régit la protection des "logiciels"
Title in Portuguese	Lei N° 9.609 de 19 de Fevereiro de 1998 dipsõe sobre a proteção de propriedade intelectual de programa de computador, sua comercialização no País, e dá outras providências
Title in Spanish	Ley N° 9.609, del 19 de febrero de 1998, que regula la protección del "programa de computador"

Figure 6: Example from CLEA

CLEA is a good example of a quality site. The above record shows that the researcher can find out the following information: name and number of law, the date of the basic text, entry into force date, the citation to the official source (here it is cited to the *Diario Oficial* for Brazil), links to related law, and links to the text in English. Not all free collections will be as organized or provide as much information as CLEA.

Case law is the hardest item to locate in both the vernacular and in translation. Keep in mind that in civil law countries, case law is not a source of primary law and there may not be any official publication of decisions. Also, in some countries, only the country's highest court will publicly issue its decisions. If you need to decipher a case citation, one of the best sources to use is *Noble's International al Guide to the Law Reports* (2002).

There really is no one source for case law (print or electronic), even from a specific jurisdiction. To locate reporters, both official and unofficial, check the sections on "Court Reports" in *Foreign Law Guide*. This section will tell you whether the country issues official reports or if you must look in other sources, such as periodicals. In many countries, legal periodicals act as unofficial sources for court decisions. Even articles in journal literature can be of assistance. For example, in the *Asian International Arbitration Journal*, there is an overview of recent Chinese cases.[27]

A few sources for translated cases include *International Law Reports* (1919–), *International Labour Law Reports* (1978–), *Bulletin on Constitutional Case–Law* (1993–)[28] and the *East European Case Reporter of Constitutional Law* (1994–). Some compilations focus on a single jurisdiction, prominent sets include *The First Ten Years of the Korean Constitutional Court: 1988–1998* (2001), *The Constitutional Jurisprudence of the Federal Republic of Germany* (2nd ed., 1997), or *Selected Judgments of*

27. Kong Yuan, *Recent Cases Relating to Arbitration in China*, 2 ASIAN INT'L. ARB. J. 179 (2006).

28. Available online via Codices Database, http://www. venice.coe.int/site/main/ CODICES_E.asp.

the Supreme Court of Israel (1962–). A new addition is Oxford's International Law in Domestic Courts.[29] This database provides English translations of selected national cases dealing with a variety of international law topics, such as human rights, trade, treaties, etc.

Some cases are translated and freely available on the web. You can locate some of these sources by consulting the research guides mentioned above. Some examples of the kinds of sites available include WorldLII Courts & Case–Law[30] and Refugee Caselaw Site.[31] WorldLII is a directory of websites organized by country, whereas Refugee Caselaw is a database containing cases related to refugee law from several different jurisdictions. Some sites provide access to selected decisions in English. For example, the Institute for Transnational Law at the University of Texas at Austin Law School provides translated decisions for France, Germany, Israel, and Austria[32] (see Figures 8 and 9).

29. http://ildc.oxford lawreports.com, available by subscription.

30. http://www.worldlii. org/catalog/2172.html.

31. http://www. refugeecaselaw.org/.

32. http://www.utexas.edu/ law/academics/centers/ transnational/work_new/.

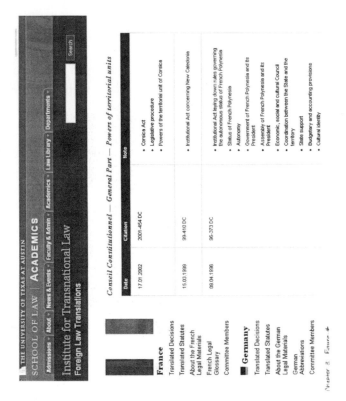

Figure 7: French Case Decisions Page

Case:
96-373 DC

Date:
09 April 1996

Translated by:
Conseil Constitutionnel

Copyright:
Conseil Constitutionnel

On 15 March 1996 the Prime Minister referred to the Constitutional Council, pursuant to Article 46 and the first paragraph of Article 61 of the Constitution, the Institutional Act laying down rules governing the autonomous status of French Polynesia;

THE CONSTITUTIONAL COUNCIL,
Having regard to the Constitution;
Having regard to Ordinance 58-1067 of 7 November 1958 laying down the Institutional Act on the Constitutional Council, as amended, and in particular Chapter II of Title II thereof;
Having regard to the Association Contract Act of 1 July 1901, as amended;
Having regard to Act 84-820 of 6 September 1984 laying down rules governing the status of the territory of French Polynesia;
Having regard to Act 85-1405 of 30 December 1985 to limit the cumulation of electoral mandates and elective offices by members of Parliament;
Having regard to Act 87-556 of 16 July 1987 transferring powers in respect of the second cycle of secondary education to the Territory of French Polynesia;
Having regard to Act 88-227 of 11 March 1988 concerning Financial transparency of political life, as amended;
Having regard to Act 90-612 of 12 July 1990 amending Act 84-820 of 6 September 1984 laying down rules governing the status of the territory of French Polynesia;
Having regard to Institutional Act 94-499 of 21 June 1994 concerning the transfer to the State of the powers of the Territory of French Polynesia in penitentiary matters;
Having regard to Institutional Act 94-1132 of 27 December 1994 concerning certain legislative provisions of Books I and II of the Code of Financial Courts;
Having regard to Institutional Act 95-173 of 20 February 1995 amending Act 88-1028 of 9 November 1988 on statutory provisions to prepare New Caledonia for self-determination in 1998 and miscellaneous provisions concerning the

Figure 8: Example of Translated French Case

There are some websites that provide national laws or codes in English. Each of these sites varies as to the number of translations provided and the focus of material chosen. For example, Legifrance provides translations of selected codes (see Figure 10).[33] FinLex contains many English translations of Finnish acts and decrees.[34] The German Law Archive has German laws in English as well as codes.[35] A final example is the Mongolian Law Library which provides a limited number of laws, including

33. http://www.legifrance. gouv.fr/html/codes_traduits/ liste.htm.

34. http://www.finlex.fi/en/.

35. http://www.iuscomp. org/gla/.

those with a focus on economic laws.[36] To locate more of these sites, see WorldLII.[37]

Figure 9: English-language Codes available from Legifrance

As business becomes more global, many more databases will emerge that provide access to foreign law in English. In fact, there are already many subscription services available, such as China Laws for Foreign Business, RIA Worldwide Tax Law, and Transnational Dispute Management.[38]

36. http://www.indiana. edu/=mongsoc/mong/lawlib. html.

37. http://www.worldlii.org /countries.html.

38. These are all subscription databases, see Appendix A for more information.

Many researchers turn to web-based translators when confronted with a page in an unfamiliar language.[39] While this is easy to do, be sure you understand that these tools can be used to help give an idea of the topic of the web document or for translating specific terms or phrases. However, use caution when using these tools because they are not always accurate.

For example, *Ley de Amparo* is an important statute in Mexican law. The *Amparo* was established to protect against "any violation or infringement of constitutional rights ... committed by an official act of public authority...."[40] The Spanish version of a section of the law is on the left side of the table below and a translated version, using Babel Fish, is on the right. As you can see, the Babel Fish translation is clearly just a literal translation and is not able to translate the terms of art contained in the statute or the nuances of the language. If you relied on the Babel Fish translation for any kind of legal document or discussion, you would be relying on faulty (and just plain wrong) information.

39. There are many such translators: Google Language Tools, http://www.google./ language_tools?hl=en, Babel Fish (Altavista), http:// babelfish.altavista.com/, and Free Online Translators, http://countriesandcities.com/ translators/. New translation services allow you to translate a section of text, see Windows Live Translator Beta, http:// translator.live.com/, and Google Translate, http://www. google.com/translate_t.

40. Jorge Vargas, *Mexican Legal Dictionary and Desk Reference* 20 (2003).

Spanish version[41]	English, translated using Babel Fish[42]
LIBRO PRIMERO Del Amparo en General	BOOK FIRST Of the Shelter in General I
TITULO PRIMERO Reglas Generales	TITLE FIRST General Rules I
CAPITULO I Disposiciones fundamentales	CAPITULATE I fundamental Dispositions
Artículo 1.-El juicio de amparo tiene por objeto resolver toda controversia que se suscite:	Article 1.-The shelter judgment intends to solve all controversy that is provoked:
I. -Por leyes o actos de la autoridad que violen las garantzías individuales;	I. -By laws or acts of the authority that violate the individual guarantees;
II. -Por leyes o actos de la autoridad federal, que vulneren o restrinjan la soberanía de los Estados;	II. -By laws or acts of the federal authority, that harm or restrict the sovereignty of the States;
III. -Por leyes o actos de las autoridades de éstos, que invadan la esfera de la autoridad federal.	III. -By laws or acts of the authorities of these, that invade the sphere of the federal authority.

Of course, when no translation exists or you need help with a single word or phrase, bilingual or multilingual dictionaries are useful tools. Most of these dictionaries related to law are not readily available on the web, but a few are available on LexisNexis. Some common dictionaries include *West's Law and Commercial Dictionary in Five Languages: Definitions of the Legal and Commercial Terms and Phrases of American, English and Civil Law Jurisdictions* (1985) and LexisNexis provides access to *Dahl's French–English Law Dictionary (2001)* and *Dahl's Spanish–English Law Dictionary (2006)*. Like online translators, dictionaries

41. http://www.asa.gob.mx/ServletRepositorio?id=22.

42. Text from site noted in footnote 40 translated using

Babel Fish, http://babelfish.altavista.com/.

do not provide any context for the terms being used. However, unlike online translators, they are geared for legal communication. Once again, check with your librarian concerning which dictionaries are available to you.

3.7 Comparative Law

As mentioned above, comparative law is a form of study and not a body of law. Comparative law books and materials present information in several different ways. Some focus on comparing legal families or traditions (civil law versus common law, ancient law, etc.). Some books compare specific countries (German law as compared to French law). Others focus on comparing topics within laws and within countries (constitutional law in Germany and the U.S.). And some sources do all of the above.

Researching comparative law usually means looking for foreign law and any related commentary. Use the tools outlined above on locating foreign law and information about foreign legal systems. Some handy sources to start with are available, but only in print. See the *Oxford Handbook of Comparative Law* (Mathias Reimann & Reinhard Zimmermann eds., 2006)[43] and the *Elgar Encyclopedia of Compar-*

43. The table of contents includes: Part 1. The development of comparative law in the world. France. Germany, Switzerland, and Austria. Italy. Great Britain. United States. Central and Eastern Europe. East Asia. Latin America—Part 2. Approaches to comparative law. Comparative law and comparative knowledge. The functional method of comparative law. Comparative law: study of similarities or differences? Comparative legal families and

ative Law (Jan M. Smits ed., 2006). For more information on this topic, see *Comparative Law in the 21st Century* (Andrew Harding & Esin Örücü eds., 2002), Werner Menski, *Comparative Law in a Global Context: The Legal Systems of Asia and Africa* (2nd ed. 2006), and Mary Ann Glendon et al., *Comparative Legal Traditions in a Nutshell* (2nd ed. 1999).

While most of the sources listed above are print, some online tools include a collection of guides on comparative law, including one on comparative criminal procedure and researching African law.[44]

There is a whole collection of comparative law journals and lots of articles in other journals on comparative law issues. There are even some electronic journals. For example, the *Electronic Journal of Comparative Law* (EJCL), which publishes articles relating to comparative private law, comparative legal aspects of information technology and the methodology of comparative law.[45] Another one is the *German Law Journal* reporting on German and European legal developments.[46] And, more recently, the *European Journal of Legal Studies*; this new

comparative legal traditions. Comparative law as the study of transplants and receptions. Comparative law and the study of mixed legal systems. Comparative law and its influence on national legal systems. Comparative law and the Europeanization of private law. Globalization and comparative law. Comparative law and the

Islamic (Middle Eastern) legal culture ...—Part 3. Subject areas.

44. http://www. nyulawglobal.org/globalex/ index.html.

45. http://www.ejcl.org/.

46. http://www.germanlaw Journal.com/index.php.

journal focuses on "overlapping national, international, and supranational legal systems."[47] For more information on locating journal articles, please see Chapter 10 of this Nutshell.

47. http://www.ejls.eu/ index.php?; see Mission Statement.

CHAPTER 4

TREATIES AND INTERNATIONAL AGREEMENTS

4.1 Introduction

Locating the text of a treaty and researching information about a treaty is one of the most common types of international legal research. While many treaties are readily available on the web, some agreements may only be available in print sources. This is especially true when looking for an older agreement or if you need a more obscure agreement between two countries. It is important to note that not all countries make treaties and agreements available on government websites.

4.2 Some Basics

Treaties can be referred to by a number of different names: international conventions, international agreements, covenants, final acts, charters, protocols, pacts, accords, and constitutions for international organizations. Usually these different names have no legal significance in international law. Treaties may be bilateral (between two parties) or multilateral (among several parties) and are usually only binding on the parties to the agreement. An agreement "enters into force" when the terms for entry into force as specified in the agreement are met. Bilateral treaties usually enter into force when both parties agree to be bound as of a certain date.

Much of the structure and rules about treaty making are set forth in the Vienna Convention on the Law of Treaties.[1] This treaty sets out basic definitions, identifies an authentic text, provides information on reservations, and the like.

For more basic information on treaties, see Thomas Buergenthal & Sean Murphy, *Public Inter-*

1. 1155 U.N.T.S. 331 (1969).

national Law in a Nutshell (4th ed. 2007) or *Encyclopedia of Public International Law*, 459–514 (1981–).

4.3   Getting Started

As a researcher, you are usually faced with the following treaty research problems:

- Locating the text of the treaty or agreement, including any updates.

- Obtaining status and ratification information.

- Locating the text of any reservations and declarations.

- Determining if national implementing legislation is needed and available.

- Looking at the intent of the treaty through background documents (negotiation or legislative history).

When you have the name of a treaty and need the text, your first instinct is probably to search the web using Google. While this may bring up many sites for obtaining the text of the agreement, it is not always the best way to begin treaty research. Some treaties go by a popular name or an acronym that may not be useful in a Google search. For example, if someone says find the "Hague conventions," a search on Google will retrieve about 115,-000 hits. While you will learn that there are many Hague conventions, you may not be able to determine which one is the relevant one. Since the web is such a powerful resource for locating treaties, try using some of these more targeted research tools:

ASIL Guide to Electronic Resources for International Law (ERG).[2]

The ERG is an electronic book designed to assist researchers in tackling the intricacies of international law research on the web. Each narrative chapter describes the scope of the topic, offers tips and caveats on online research and resources, and provides links to the most important and useful primary and secondary materials on the web. The ERG allows you to explore the breadth of a topic or focus on locating information on a narrow issue.

2. http://www.asil.org/resource/home.htm.

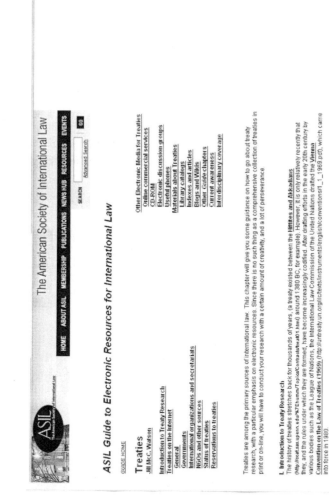

Figure 1: ASIL ERG: Treaties

Electronic Information System for International Law (EISIL).[3]

EISIL provides, in a single location, easy access to carefully selected web materials covering the entire spectrum of international law. It is designed to help you explore and understand the scope of international law under thirteen major topic headings. The database includes information on international legal instruments, websites, and other research tools and sources. EISIL allows browsing by subject, and/or search by keywords, dates and resource type.

4.4   U.S. Treaties and Agreements

A.   Background Information

Before delving into treaties too deeply, a few words about U.S. treaties and agreements are in order. "Domestically, treaties to which the United States is a party are equivalent in status to Federal legislation, forming part of what the Constitution calls 'the supreme Law of the Land.' Yet, the word treaty does not have the same meaning in the United States and in international law."[4] The Vienna Convention on the Law of Treaties defines a treaty "as an international agreement concluded

---

3. http://www.eisil.org/.

4. *Treaties and Other International Agreements: The Role of the United States Senate: A Study*, prepared for the Committee on Foreign Relations, United States Senate, S. Print 106–71, at 1(2001), available at http://frwebgate.access.gpo.gov/cgi-bin/getdoc.cgi?dbname=106_cong_senate_print&docid=f:66922.pdf.

between States in written form and governed by international law, whether embodied in a single instrument or in two or more related instruments and whatever its particular designation."[5] Under United States law, however, there is a distinction between the terms *treaty* and *executive agreement.* "In the United States, the word treaty is reserved for an agreement that is made 'by and with the Advice and Consent of the Senate' (Article II, section 2, clause 2 of the Constitution). International agreements not submitted to the Senate are known as 'executive agreements' in the United States."[6] Regardless of whether an international agreement is called a convention, agreement, protocol, accord, etc., if it is submitted to the Senate for advice and consent, it is considered a treaty under United States law.

A common misconception is that all U.S. treaties and agreements are freely available on the web. While there are collections of instruments, there is no one comprehensive collection for them all.

1. Full-text Sources

Until 1950, U.S. treaties appeared regularly after proclamation in *Statutes at Large* (1789–). Pre–1950 treaties can also be found in *Treaties and Other International Agreements of the United States of*

---

5. Vienna Convention on the Law of Treaties, 1155 U.N.T.S. 311 (May 23, 1969), art. 2, s 1(a), available at http://untreaty.un.org/ilc/texts/ instruments/english/conven tions/1_1_1969.pdf.

6. *Treaties and Other International Agreements: The Role of the United States Senate: A Study,* supra note 4.

America, 1776–1949 (1968–1976). This 13–volume set is commonly cited by the compilers' name, Bevans. In 1950, *United States Treaties and Other International Agreements* (cited as U.S.T.) (1950–) became the official source for all U.S. treaties and agreements. Several volumes are published annually, each with a non-cumulative subject and country index. Note that there is currently more than a 20 year lag time between ratification and official publication in U.S.T.

U.S. treaties first appear in slip form in *Treaties and Other International Acts Series* (cited as T.I.A.S.) (1946–), a set of individually paginated pamphlets, consecutively numbered. This series has a lag time of 8–9 years. Before ratification, check on the status of a treaty in *CCH Congressional Index* (1938–) or on the U.S. Senate website.

After ratification, but still well before treaties appear in slip form, selected treaties (after they are cleared for publication by the Senate) are published in the *Senate Treaty Document Series* (1981–)(formerly the *Senate Executive Document Series*).[7] Pursuant to Public Law 108–458,[8] the Secretary of State is required to publish on the State Department's website "each treaty or international agreements proposed to be published in the compilation 'United States Treaties and Other International Agreements' not later than 180 days after the date

7. Senate Treaty Documents are available on the web from the 104th Congress to present, http://www.gpoaccess. gov/serialset/cdocuments/index.html.

8. 11 Stat. 3638, 3807 (2004).

on which the treaty or agreement enters into force." This collection begins with 1998.[9]

2. Treaty Indexes

There are several indexes and guides that provide citations to treaties and agreements where the U.S. is a party. The most common is *Treaties in Force*, (TIF), published by the U.S. Department of State. This annual publication lists and provides basic information for all U.S. treaties and agreements in force. It is arranged by country and subject and includes both bilateral and multilateral treaties and provides citations to U.S.T. and T.I.A.S. (if they are available). The primary use of TIF is verification of the existence of a treaty. While TIF is also available on the web, the electronic version is usually no more current than the print.[10] Since TIF is only published once a year, use *Treaty Actions* to update TIF.[11] The problem with *Treaty Actions* is that they are not always up to date. TIF is also available on LexisNexis and Westlaw. Where possible, TIF on LexisNexis and Westlaw links to the text of the treaty. Archived editions of TIF are available on HeinOnline from 1955 to present.

9. http://www.foia.state. gov/SearchColls/CollsSearch. asp. (Note: In June 2007, The State Department removed its collection of international agreements from the Freedom of Information Act Electronic Reading Room page. Agree-ments are now available at http://www.state.gov/m/a/ips/ c24150.htm.)

10. http://www.state.gov/s/ l/treaty/.

11. http://www.state.gov/s/ l/treaty/c3428.htm.

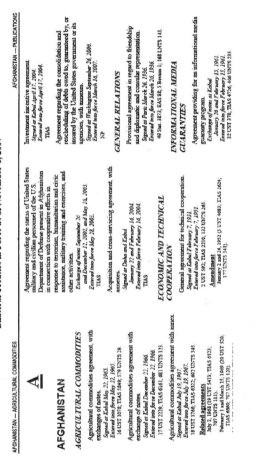

Figure 2: *Treaties in Force*

Because TIF is not always satisfactory for treaty research, there are some other tools available. *A Guide to the United States Treaties in Force* (I.

Kavass and A. Sprudzs, eds., 1982–) is an annual publication and should be used in conjunction with TIF. Access is by a combined subject index for both bilateral and multilateral treaties, as well as by numerical and country index. This guide is also available on HeinOnline. It is supplemented by *Guide to the United States Treaties in Force: Current Treaty Action Supplement.*

Also published by Hein is the *United States Treaty Index* (15 vols.) (I. Kavass, ed., 1991–). This is one of the most comprehensive sources for U.S. treaty information. There are subject, chronological, and country indexes. This set is supplemented by *Current Treaty Index*, (I. Kavass and A. Sprudzs, eds., 1982–), a looseleaf index listing current treaties and agreements published in slip form in T.I.A.S. as well as those treaties without T.I.A.S. numbers. The treaties are available on microfiche in *Hein's United States Treaties and Other International Agreements* and on HeinOnline.

Another good treaty tool is Thomas: Treaties. This web collection provides some information for locating treaty documents from 90th Congress to the present. Search by Congress, treaty document number, word/phrase, or by type of treaty. Some full-text treaties are available.[12]

Many of these same tools can be used to obtain status and ratification information. For example, TIF is a good source for determining which treaties and agreements are in force for the United States.

12.   http://thomas.loc.gov/ home/treaties/treaties.htm.

3.   Other Full-text Sources

Because the official publication of U.S. treaties and agreements is slow, other sources have filled the gap. Treaties are available on LexisNexis, Westlaw, Treaties and International Agreements Online,[13] and HeinOnline.[14] Each of these databases provides access to many of the treaties and agreements, but none of these services is complete on its own.

As noted above, selected treaties and agreements are freely available on the web. The State Department makes a number of agreements available including bilateral investment treaties,[15] nonproliferation treaties,[16] and verification and compliance agreements.[17] Other federal government agencies provide access to agreements, such the U.S. Department of Commerce, Trade and Related Agreements Database,[18] Trade Agreements Library from the U.S. Trade Representative,[19] and U.S. Income Tax Treaties from the IRS.[20]

13. http://www.oceanalaw. com (subscription only).

14. http://heinonline.org/ HOL/Index?collection=us treaties&set_as_cursor= clear (subscription only).

15. http://www.state.gov/e/ eeb/rls/fs/2006/22422.htm.

16. http://www.state.gov/t/ isn/trty/.

17. http://www.state.gov/t/ vci/trty/.

18. http://tcc.export.gov/ Trade_Agreements/index.asp.

19. http://www.ustr.gov/ Trade_Agreements/Section_ Index.html.

20. http://www.irs.gov/ businesses/international/ article/0,,id=96739,00.html.

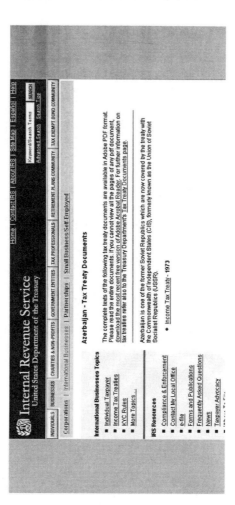

Figure 3: IRS Tax Treaty Page

4.5　Bilateral and Multilateral Treaties and Agreements

A.　Bilateral Treaties

Locating bilateral treaties where the U.S. is not a party can be more challenging. Many bilateral agreements are published in the *United Nations Treaty Series* (cited as U.N.T.S.). Nevertheless, you may still need to look at collections by country or topic.

Some countries do publish a treaty series, such as the *Australian Treaty Series*.[21] Other countries publish treaties in an official gazette.[22] However, most researchers will not have access to these print collections. Several countries have made their treaties available on the web or in its official gazette. An outstanding model for making treaties available is the Australian Treaties Library.[23] To locate other such collections, consult the WorldLII collection of treaties by country[24] and the Foreign Treaties section of Foreign and International Law Resources: An Annotated Guide to Web Sites Around the World.[25]

21. Available on the web at http://www.austlii.edu.au/au/other/dfat/treaties/.

22. Official gazettes are published by a government and are often the primary mechanism for distributing laws. Some of these publications are available on the web, see Government Gazettes Online, http://www.lib.umich.edu/govdocs/gazettes/index.htm.

23. http://www.austlii.edu.au/au/other/dfat/.

24. http://www.worldlii.org/catalog/2322.html.

25. http://www.law.harvard.edu/library/services/

B. Multilateral Treaties

1. Indexes

Multilateral Treaties Deposited with the Secretary General (1982–) is a good source for citations and a list of the parties to an agreement. It is limited to those treaties deposited with the U.N. An electronic version is also available on the U.N. Treaty Collection on the web.[26]

One of the most complete treaty indexes, at least for the time period covered, is Christian L. Wiktor, *Multilateral Treaty Calendar = Repertoire des Traites Multilateraux, 1648–1995* (1998). This hefty volume provides citation information, treaty depository, and information about later related treaties and amendments.

2. Full-text Sources

There are many sources for the full text of multi-lateral treaties, both print and electronic. Some of the primary print historical collections include the *Consolidated Treaty Series* (cited as C.T.S.) (1969–1986) covers 1648–1918 and the *League of Nations Treaty Series* (cited as L.N.T.S.) (1920–1946) which covers 1920–1944. L.N.T.S. is also available on the U.N. Treaty Collection database.[27] Be sure to select the "advanced search" option so you can limit the search to this collection.

research/guides/international/
web_resources/treaties.php

26. http://untreaty.un.org/ English/access.asp. This site is now freely available, but is frozen as of late 2007, until the new site is launched

27. http://untreaty.un.org/.

The *United Nations Treaty Series* (cited as U.N.T.S.) covers 1944–date and is one of the most important treaty collections. Most, if not all, of the treaties contained in this source are also contained within the U.N. Treaty Collection website. This collection does have a lag time of a couple of years.

Since not all treaties are deposited with the U.N., there are other international organizations which publish treaties done under the auspices of the organization. For example, the Council of Europe publishes the *European Treaty Series* (1949–) and *European Conventions and Agreements* (1971–). The Organization of American States publishes a *Treaty Series* (1956–) as well. Many of these organizations have websites that contain the text of these treaties, see the Web Treaty Collections, Appendix B.

Other sources for treaties include periodicals, looseleaf services or subject compilations, such as *International Law & World Order: Basic Documents* (1994–), *International Documents on Children* (2nd ed. 1998) or *Investment Promotion and Protection Treaties* (1983–). Some compilations may focus on a region and a topic, such as *European Taxation: Supplementary Service* (1963–) or *Latin American Trade Agreements* (1997–). These topical collections may also contain bilateral treaties.

Once the text of the treaty has been located, the next piece of information needed is to determine the parties, ratifications and reservations. This can be the most difficult information to locate for many treaties. The information differs depending on the country or the body named as the depository (the custodian of the treaty). The depository is usually indicated in the final article of the treaty, and the depository functions are detailed in Article 77 of the Vienna Convention on the Law of Treaties.

The web has become one of the most important sources for status and ratification information from treaty secretariats, national ministries, and international organizations. Other electronic tools, such as the United Nations Treaty Collection, are also good for getting status information. See Appendix B for websites containing status and ratification information.

RUDs are reservations, understandings, and declarations. Reservations exclude or modify the legal effect of provisions; understandings and declarations clarify a State's position. Some treaties prohibit reservations or only permit specified reservations; see articles 2(1)(d) and 19–23 of the Vienna Convention on the Law of Treaties. Declarations and understandings are unilateral statements that clarify a State's position and do not change or modify the binding nature of the treaty provisions. Many of the same sources for status and ratification information also provide access to RUDs.

4.6   Implementing Legislation

Treaties may be "self-executing" (those that do not require implementing legislation and become effective as domestic law as soon as they enter into force) and other treaties may be non-self-executing and require "implementing legislation." Implementing legislation may require a new domestic law or changes to an existing law (technically, the legislation is the domestic law and not the treaty).

It is important to note that it is not always clear whether a treaty is self-executing or requires implementing legislation. Some treaties contain a provision calling for implementing legislation. In the U.S., the Executive Branch often decides whether or not a treaty requires such legislation. However, on occasion, the Senate includes an understanding in the resolution of ratification stating that certain provisions are not self-executing or that the President is to exchange or deposit the instrument of ratification only after implementation legislation has been enacted.

To locate implementing legislation, consult sources of domestic legislation for the country in question. Some treaty secretariats provide such information. For example, see the secretariat's website for the Chemical Weapons Convention[28] or the OECD's Anti–Bribery Convention: National Implementing Legislation.[29]

4.7 Background Information, Commentary, Treaty Interpretation and "Travaux Préparatoires"

Researching the background or history of non-U.S. treaties is challenging, especially for bilateral

28. http://www.opcw.org/.

29. http://www.oecd.org/document/30/0,2340,en_2649_

34859_2027102_1_1_1_1,00.html.

treaties. For the most part, you will not have access to materials for a legislative history for other countries. If you are researching the background of a multilateral treaty, many more resources are available.

Look for "travaux préparatoires" or history and commentaries in library catalogs or use journal indexes. For example, see *Travaux Préparatoires of the Fair Trial Provisions—Articles 8 to 11—of the Universal Declaration of Human Rights*, 21 HUM. RTS. Q. 1061 (1999) or *Guide to the Travaux Préparatoires of the United Nations Convention on the Elimination of all Forms of Discrimination against Women* (1993). For more information on how to research the history of a treaty, see À la Recherche des Travaux Préparatoires: An Approach to Researching the Drafting History of International Agreements by Jonathan Pratter.[30]

If the treaty or agreement was concluded pursuant to an international conference, look for conference documents using the name of the conference as an author or subject in a library catalog. If it is a recent conference, try searching for the conference on the web. For example, the United Nations Framework Convention on Climate Change website provides access to documents, national reports, and other up–to-date information.[31]

30. http://www. nyulawglobal.org/globalex/ Travaux_Preparatoires.htm.

31. http://unfccc.int/2860. php.

If the treaty or conference was done under the auspices of an international organization, such as the U.N., look for documents using tools for locating such documents. See the United Nations Documentation: Research Guide[32] for U.N. documents and the ASIL Guide to Electronic Resources for International Law: International Organizations[33] for tips on researching IGOs and NGOs on the web.

If you want to research how treaties are implemented or interpreted in domestic legal systems, the most useful tools include books on the topics, international law yearbooks, *International Law Reports* (1919–) (a compilation of selected international and domestic court decisions), and the database International Law in Domestic Courts (domestic caselaw on international law issues).[34]

32. http://www.un.org/Depts/dhl/resguide/.

33. http://www.asil.org/resource/intorg1.htm.

34. http://ildc.oxfordreports.com (subscription database).

CHAPTER 5

CUSTOMARY INTERNATIONAL LAW AND GENERAL PRINCIPLES OF LAW

5.1 Introduction

According to Article 38(1)(b) and (c) of the International Court of Justice Statute, customary international law and general principles of law are two of the major sources of international law. Neither of these "sources of law" will sound familiar to a non-specialist. But it you consider the matter for a second, they are natural locations for authority in international law. Nations have been dealing with each other for millennia. For all of the faults that one can find with international law, an amazing amount of international law works fine and it has done so for centuries. Travel, trade, communications and diplomacy, the list could go on and on. As long as there have been nations, there have been ways in which nations dealt with one another. It makes sense that some of these deep-rooted concepts have taken on the force of law. Perhaps no one can pinpoint when a custom began, or when it became accepted. The important point is that it is accepted as the governing rule.

This type of authority is not really so different from the idea of the Common Law, it is just more complex because it springs from the interaction of many nations and traditions. Nor is it always clear just what customary international law and general principles of law might be. Naturally, these are also the two most difficult sources to research. They are documented in a wide variety of sources and often involve very subjective evaluation. This Chapter will try to help guide you, but in this area, asking for help from a librarian or a more experienced researcher may be the best solution.

Article 38(1)(d) also mentions judicial decisions and the teachings of publicists as "subsidiary means for the determination of rules of law." Case law and teachings are not primary sources of law, but they do provide evidence of the primary sources of international law. These forms of authority are familiar to the modern American researcher, though knowing which publicists (which means scholarly commentators) are central is just a matter of learning about them. We will provide a list of the most widely accepted sources at the end of the Chapter.

5.2 Customary International Law

Some basic definitions will help. Customary international law "consists of rules of law derived from the consistent conduct of States acting out of the belief that the law required them to act that way."[1] The elements of customary international law include:

- Widespread repetition by States of similar international acts over time. This is referred to as "state practice." In other words, "everyone has always done it this way."

- Acts must occur out of a sense of obligation, called *opinio juris*. In other words, "everyone has always done it this way because they knew they were supposed to do so."

- Acts must be taken by a significant number of States and not be rejected by a significant number of States. Of course there is no magic number here. In other words, "when we say everyone, we mean a real consensus."

The *Restatement (Third) of Foreign Relations* states in a straightforward manner: "[c]ustomary international law results from a general and consistent practice of states followed by them from a sense of legal obligation."[2]

"Customary international law develops from the practice of States. To international lawyers, 'the

1. Shabtai Rosenne, *Practice and Methods of International Law* 55(1984).

2. Rest. 3d FOREL § 102, available on LexisNexis and Westlaw.

practice of states' means official governmental conduct reflected in a variety of acts, including official statements at international conferences and in diplomatic exchanges, formal instructions to diplomatic agents, national court decisions, legislative measures or other actions taken by governments to deal with matters of international concern."[3]

5.3 State Practice

When doing research in this area, the objective is to find evidence of the relevant State practice. Evidence of State practice is found in a variety of primary source materials. In 1950, the International Law Commission listed the following as evidence of customary international law: treaties, decisions of national and international courts, national legislation, opinions of national legal advisors, diplomatic correspondence, and practice of international organizations. This list, which was not intended to be exhaustive, is useful as a starting point and a basis for discussion.[4]

One of the best sources of State practice is the records of a State's foreign relations and diplomatic practices. However, for many States, this information is quite a challenge to obtain because they are

3. Buergenthal, Thomas & Sean Murphy, *Public International Law in a Nutshell* 22–23 (2007).

4. "Report of the International Law Commission to the General Assembly (Part II): Ways and Means of Making the Evidence of Customary International Law More Readily Available," [1950] 2 *Y.B. Int'l L. Comm'n* 367, ILC Doc. A/1316.

generally not available to the public. It may come as a surprise to the neophyte that such compilations exist at all, but it is a tradition for nation's to produce such tools. For the United States, the best source is the series called *Foreign Relations of the United States* (1861–). The *Foreign Relations of the United States* series "presents the official documentary historical record of major U.S. foreign policy decisions and significant diplomatic activity."[5] The series began in 1861 and consists of hundreds of individual volumes. The volumes contain documents from Presidential libraries, Departments of State and Defense, National Security Council, Central Intelligence Agency, Agency for International Development, and other foreign affairs agencies as well as the private papers of individuals involved in formulating U.S. foreign policy. It represents an amazingly detailed account of the international activity of the United States. You will not be surprised to discover that this set appears with elegant slowness. Due to declassification rules, the compilers of this set are just getting started on the activities of the Nixon/ Ford administrations.

Researchers can now obtain many of these volumes on the web. The University of Wisconsin has digitized 1861–1958/1960 (372 vols.).[6] The State Department has put up selected volumes from the Truman, Eisenhower, Kennedy, Johnson, Nixon, and Ford administrations.[7] HeinOnline, which is

5. http://www.state.gov/r/pa/ho/frus/.

6. http://digicoll.library.wisc.edu/FRUS/.

7. http://www.state.gov/r/pa/ho/frus/.

available in many law libraries, has the most complete collection from 1861 to 1976.[8]

Other more current documents and bits of information are available in the *Department of State Bulletin* (1939–1989) and the *Dispatch* (1990–1999). Both of these publications contain documentation and information from the Department of State and provide a wealth of information on foreign relations. Unfortunately, the State Department discontinued publication of these sources in 1999. The same information that was contained in the two former tools is supposedly available on the website of the State Department, but locating it is now a bit more challenging.[9]

A good source for locating sources of State practice for a number of countries is *Sources of State Practice in International Law* (Gaebler & Smolka–Day eds., 2001–). For each country included in this volume, there is information on treaty collections, diplomatic and state papers, and other sources. This is a fine place to start.

Many countries have websites for departments or ministries that serve the same function as the U.S. Department of State, e.g. the United Kingdom's Foreign and Commonwealth Office,[10] Australia's Department of Foreign Affairs and Trade,[11] and Germany's Auswärtiges Amt.[12] What you find at each site will vary from country to country.

8. http://heinonline.org.

9. http://www.state.gov/.

10. http://www.fco.gov.uk/.

11. http://www.dfat.gov.au/.

12. http://www.auswaertiges-amt.de/diplo/de/Startseite.html.

International law digests are another useful source. Digests aid in locating customary international law contained in diplomatic papers of States. The easiest to access are the digests for the United States. For historical information, there are many digests covering the late 19th century and the 20th century: Cadwalader, *Digest of Published Opinions of the Attorneys–General and of the Leading Decisions of the Federal Courts, with Reference to International Law, Treaties, and Kindred Subjects* (1877); Wharton, *Digest of the International Law of the United States* (1886); Moore, *Digest of International Law* (1906); Hackworth, *Digest of International Law* (1940–1944); and Whiteman, *Digest of International Law* (1963–1973). These digests are also available on HeinOnline.[13]

More contemporary information can be located in the *Digest of United States Practice in International Law* (1973–1980; 2001–). The earlier edition was continued by *Cumulative Digest of United States Practice in International Law* (1981–) which covered 1981–1988. These volumes were supplemented monthly by a column in the *American Journal of International Law* ("Contemporary Practice of the United States Relating to International Law"). The new edition of the *Digest* began with 2000 and is issued annually. Documents listed in the *Digest* are available on the State Department's website (see Figure 1).[14] Another digest is done by Sean Murphy,

13. http://heinonline.org.   **14.** http://www.state.gov/s/l/c8183.htm.

United States Practice in International Law (2002–). It includes citations to US statutes and cases, US documents, international documents and materials.

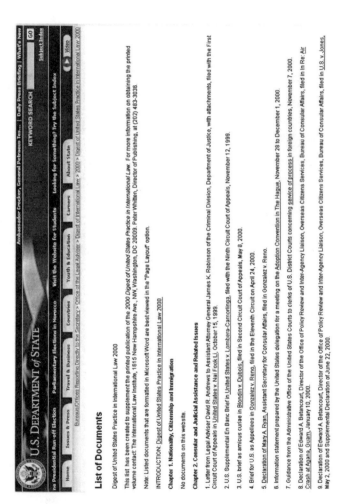

Figure 1: International Law Digest

While all of the sources noted above are important for researching customary international law, probably the best resources for US legal researchers is the *Restatement of the Law, Third, Foreign Relations* (1987–, plus supplement).[15] Like all of the Restatements, it is the distillation of the best thinking of scholars, judges and lawyers. Though it is unofficial, it possesses great authority with a focus on the U.S. but it also cites other international documents. If you do nothing else, give this Restatement a go to gain a better understanding of this source of international law. It is designed to be a rational explanation of the field. The Restatement is a reliable source of context.

A country's domestic laws also provide evidence of international custom because they indicate the State's practice and obligations. To research the law of other countries, see Chapter 3 of this Nutshell. Since locating the laws relevant to international law can be a daunting task, you should use a "yearbook" if one is available for the jurisdiction. Many countries publish an international yearbook which contains summaries or overviews of national legislation and case law dealing with that State's international obligations. These yearbooks may include cases involving questions of public international law, legislation concerning matters of international law, practice in international law, and treaty actions. At this point you will not be surprised to learn that most yearbooks lag years behind in appearing. These examples may give you an idea of the breadth of yearbooks, but there are many more available:

15. Also available on Westlaw and LexisNexis.

- *African Yearbook of International Law = Annuaire Africain de Droit International* (1994–).[16]

- *Annuaire Français de Droit International* (1955–).

- *Asian Yearbook of International Law* (1993–).*

- *Australian Yearbook of International Law* (1966–).[17]

- *German Yearbook of International Law* (1948–).[18]

- *Japanese Annual of International Law* (1957–).

- *Netherlands Yearbook of International Law* (1970–).

- *Russian Yearbook of International Law* (1994–).

- *Spanish Yearbook of International Law* (1994–).*

Intergovernmental organizations also publish yearbooks that provide an annual survey of activities. Evidence of State practice can be found in documents issued by intergovernmental organizations, such as resolutions and declarations. Resolutions are non-binding, but they reflect the acceptance of international norms. A useful way to locate this information is to use an organization's annual yearbook. Some common yearbooks include the *Max*

16. Also available on Hein Online, http://heinonline.org.

* Also available on HeinOnline, http://heinonline.org.

17. Also available on Hein Online, http://heinonline.org.

18. The Max Planck Institute for Comparative Public Law provides the text of German practice from the Yearbook from 1993–2003 (in German), http://www.mpil.de/ww/en/pub/research/details/publications/institute/prax.cfm.

Planck Yearbook of United Nations Law (1998–)*
and the United Nations International Law Commission, *Yearbook of the International Law Commission*
(1949–).

There are a few published sources that compile
State practice and, if one exists on your topic, it can
be an enormously helpful source. Some of these
include *State Practice Regarding State Immunities*
(2006); *Customary International Humanitarian Law*
(2005) (a detailed three—volume set: volume 1 contains the rules and volumes 2 & 3 contain examples
of State practice); and *Customary International Law
on the Use of Force: A Methodological Approach*
(2005). Compilations like these may be available for
other topics in journal literature. For example, El-
ferink & Johnson, *Outer Limits of the Continental
Shelf and 'Disputed Areas': State Practice concerning Article 76(10) of the LOS Convention*, 21 Int'l J.
Marine & Coastal L. 461 (2006). Check the periodical indexes discussed in Chapter 10 to find such
articles.

5.4 General Principles

Article 38 of the International Court of Justice
Statute includes "general principles of law recognized by civilized nations" as another source of
international law. General principles are basic concepts of fairness and justice which are applied uni-
versally in legal systems around the world (e.g.
laches, good faith, res judicata, impartiality of
judges). They frequently involve procedural mat-

* Also available on HeinOnline, http://heinonline.org.

ters. International tribunals rely on these principles when they cannot find authority in other sources of international law. As stated in a piece in the International Judicial Monitor, general principles "fill the gap" when no treaty or custom exits to resolve an international dispute.[19] To make this a bit more clear, Professor Janis states,

> "The basic notion is that a general principle of international law is some proposition of law so fundamental that it will be found in virtually every legal system. When treaties and customary international law fail to offer a needed international rule, a search may be launched in comparative law to discover if national legal systems use a common legal principle. If such a common legal principle is found, then it is presumed that a comparable principle should be attributed to fill the gap in international law."[20]

For the most part, there is no handy list of these principles, but you can find references in decisions of international tribunals and national courts and in the writings (or teachings) of publicists. There are a few sources that provide information on general principles, see Bin Cheng, *General Principles of Law, as applied by International Courts and Tribunals* (1953).

Article 38 also mentions "judicial decisions and the teachings of the most highly qualified publicists

19. http://www.judicial monitor.org/current/general principles.html.

20. Mark W. Janis, *An Introduction to International Law* 55 (4th ed. 2003).

of the various nations, as subsidiary means for the determination of rules of law.'' These sources are generally the best place to start researching an international law topic since they can help you identify rules in other sources of international law, such as treaties. Scholarly works include treatises, journal articles, publications of scholarly associations, and articles in international law encyclopedias.

The writings of publicists can be found in most law libraries and even non-specialized collections. As with general principles, there is no official list of who is considered a publicist and who is not. The most prominent specialists will vary from topic to topic. However, here are some recognized classics:

Bowett's Law of International Institutions (Philippe Sands; Pierre Klein; D. W. Bowett, eds., 5th ed. 2001).

J.L. Brierly, *Law of Nations: An Introduction to the International Law of Peace* (6th ed. 1963).

Ian Brownlie, *Principles of Public International Law* (6th ed., 2003).

Mark W. Janis, *An Introduction to International Law* (4th ed. 2003)

L. Oppenheim, *Oppenheim's International Law* (Robert Jennings and Arthur Watts, eds., 9th ed. 1992).

Peter Malanczuk, *Akehurst's Modern Introduction to International Law* (8th rev. ed. 2002).

Malcolm Shaw, *International Law* (5th ed. 2003).

Gerhard von Glahn & James Larry Taulbee, *Law Among Nations: An Introduction to Public International Law* (8th ed. 2007).

Encyclopedia of Public International Law (1981–1990; 1992–).

Judicial decisions are good for finding references to and recognition of rules in other sources of law, such as treaties. To locate the decisions of international courts and tribunals, see Chapter 6.

For more assistance with researching customary international law and general principles, try using another guide called Researching Customary International Law, State Practice and the Pronouncements of States regarding International Law.[21]

As a final thought, never hesitate to ask for help. A reference librarian who works with international materials may be able to point you in the right direction, saving you time and energy. This is an area where there is no substitute for expertise.

21. http://www. nyulawglobal.org/globalex/ Customary_International_ Law.htm.

CHAPTER 6

INTERNATIONAL CASE LAW

6.1　Introduction

Judicial decisions are the bread and butter of research for the American legal researcher. The same is not true for research in international law. Since there is no single source of authority to enforce the judgments of an international tribunal, international case law has never been as central to the research enterprise. But as globalization continues, the role for decision-making bodies grows. This is a trend that is likely to continue.

Thus, it is not surprising that dispute resolution mechanisms have become of great interest to the international legal researcher. The beginning researcher must recognize that there are a variety of bodies involved in solving international disputes: international courts and tribunals, arbitral bodies, and other quasi-judicial bodies. Some look and act familiar; some do not. Fortunately, the Project on International Courts and Tribunals has produced a "synoptic chart" which provides you with a snapshot of all of these bodies.[1] Some of these mechanisms are developed for a particular dispute or event and some are proscribed based on a topic or an organization. Also, some of these bodies allow both States and individuals to bring matters before these bodies. Most of these bodies have jurisdiction based on authority outlined in an international agreement. With each tribunal or court that you examine, you will have to turn a new page and be sure that you understand what you are working with at the time. It is no surprise that there is much discussion on the effectiveness of these bodies.

6.2 Judicial Decisions of International Tribunals

There is really only one court that has general jurisdiction that, at least in theory, runs throughout all of the nations of the word—the International Court of Justice (ICJ) and its predecessor, the Permanent Court of International Justice (PCIJ). Just

1. http://www.pict-pcti.org/ publications/synoptic_chart/ synoptic_chart2.pdf.

keep in mind that there is no entity that can enforce the judgment of these courts.

A. Permanent Court of International Justice (PCIJ)

The PCIJ operated from 1920–1945/46, and it heard 66 cases, including 36 contentious cases between States and 27 advisory opinions.[2] While there is a large print collection containing all of the relevant documents, the ICJ website contains all of the PCIJ documents that used to only be available in print.[3]

Selected cases from the PCIJ are also available from the WorldLII Project on International Courts & Tribunals.[4] The advantage of this database is its superior search mechanism. Information about the PCIJ, including its history, structure, procedure, jurisdiction, and statistics are available on another website called Worldcourts.com.[5] This site also has decisions, including judgments, advisory opinions, and orders.

2. http://www.worldcourts. com/pcij/eng/statistics/general statistics.htm.

3. http://www.icj-cij.org/ pcij/index.php?p1=9.

4. http://www.worldlii.org/ int/cases/PCIJ/.

5. http://www.worldcourts. com/pcij/eng/index.htm.

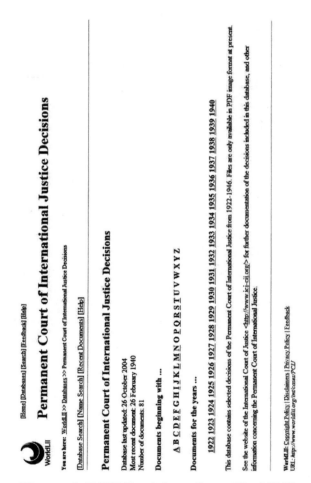

Figure 1: PCIJ Decisions from WorldLII

B. International Court of Justice (ICJ)

"The Court has a twofold role: to settle, in accordance with international law, legal disputes submitted to it by States (contentious cases) and to give advisory opinions (advisory proceedings) on legal questions referred to it by duly authorized United Nations organs and specialized agencies."[6] The ICJ website contains all of the decisions of the court, although some are only in summary form. Five series of publications are accessible on the site (as well as print): 1) Reports of Judgments, Advisory Opinions and Orders; 2) Pleadings, Oral Arguments, Documents; 3) Acts and Documents; 4) Yearbooks; and 5) Bibliography.

Basic documents, such as the Statute and Rules of the Court, are also available. Prof. Claire Germain's International Court of Justice Research Guide is available on the Cornell Law Library website and provides guidance on researching the ICJ.[7] It provides useful context and background. The decisions and documents are also available on Westlaw and LexisNexis.

6. http://www.icj-cij.org/ docket/index.php?p1=3.

7. http://library.lawschool. cornell.edu/WhatWeDo/ ResearchGuides/ICJ.cfm.

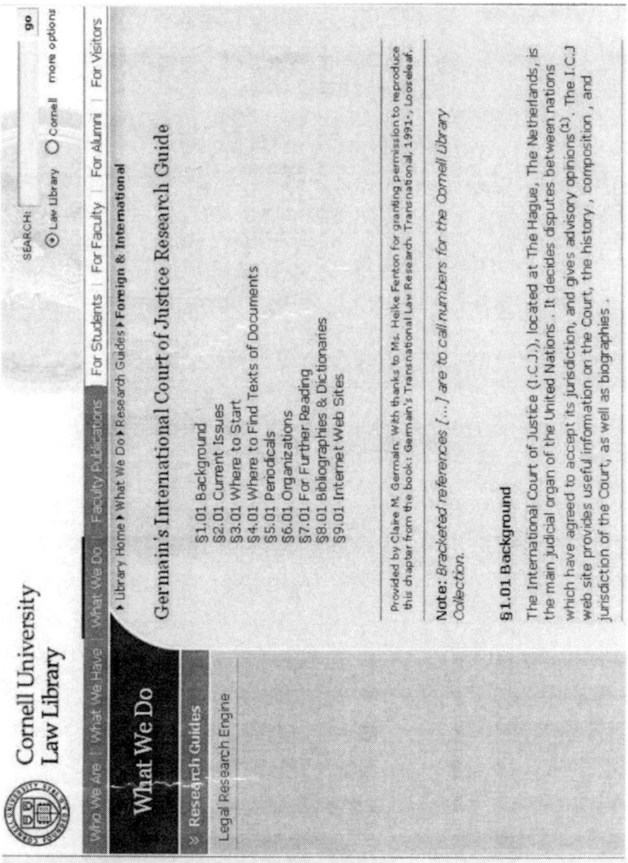

Figure 2: Germain's ICJ Research Guide

There is a considerable amount commentary and analysis on the ICJ. Some notable ones include: *The Statute of the International Court of Justice: A Commentary* (Andreas Zimmermann et al. eds., 2006) and Shabtai Rosenne, *The Law and Practice of the International Court, 1920–2005* (4th ed. 2006).

C.   Court of Justice of the European Union (ECJ)

As discussed in Chapter 7, another important court is the one that decides cases that arise within the European Union. The European Court of Justice is the highest legal authority in the EU. The Court is empowered to decide cases involving interpretation and application of the EU foundational treaties. Unlike the ICJ, this Court can enforce its decisions. EU institutions and Member States may appeal and take each other to Court for failure to implement or properly apply the treaties and secondary legislation (for example, the Commission can file a case against a Member State for not implementing a directive). The Court will also issue prejudicial decisions in cases referred to it by national courts when questions of Community law are involved. The Court is assisted by advocate-generals, who present a reasoned and independent opinion of the issue of law in the case. While there is no formal doctrine of stare decisis applied to these opinions, the Court tends to follow its own decisions. The decisions are binding on the national courts of Member States. In 1989, the Court of First Instance began hearing disputes between Community civil servants and their institutions, actions in the field of competition law, actions under anti-dumping law, and actions under the Treaty establishing the European Coal and Steel Community

(ECSC) Treaty. In 2005, the disputes between the civil servants and the Community institutions were moved to the Civil Service Tribunal.

The Court's website (called Curia[8]) provides access to all case law since 1953. Because of the changes to the Courts, there are three groups of cases: 1) Cases before the ECJ (1953–1988, 1989–); 2) Cases before the Court of First Instance (1989–); and 3) Cases before the Civil Service Tribunal (2005–). The Court's website provides access to cases by number or through a search engine. However, the search mechanism on the site only covers cases since June 17, 1997. Earlier cases can be searched using Eur–Lex[9] (covered in Chapter 7). Other tools on this site for locating cases are only available in French. Both Westlaw and LexisNexis provide searchable access to the Court's cases.

8. http://curia.europa.eu/en/transitpage.htm.

9. http://europa.eu.int/eur-lex/lex/en/index.htm.

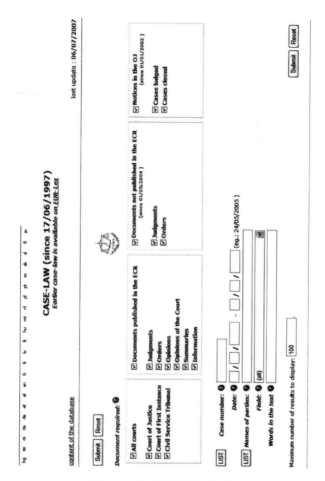

Figure 3: ECJ Website

It's important to note that researchers needing authentic versions of the Court's jurisprudence must use the version published in *Reports of Cases before the Court* (1959-1989), also called *European Court Reports* (1990–). See the note on the Court's website in Figure 3 below.

For the benefit of the public, the electronic version of the texts of the three Community courts is available free of charge on Internet for information purposes. This version is subject to amendment. The definitive version of these texts will be published in the "Reports of Cases before the Court of Justice and the Court of First Instance", the "Reports of European Community Staff Cases" or the "Official Journal of the European Union" which alone are authentic and, in the event of their differing from the electronic version, are alone to be regarded as authoritative. Reproduction of the texts supplied on this site is authorised provided that their source and non-authentic character are acknowledged and it is mentioned that they have been provided free of charge.

Figure 4: Notice on Court's Website

D. European Court of Human Rights (ECHR)

The most active of all of the human rights courts and bodies is the ECHR. The European Convention on Human Rights established a mechanism for the enforcement of the obligations entered into by Contracting States. Initially, there were three institutions entrusted with this responsibility: the European Commission of Human Rights (1954–1998), the European Court of Human Rights (1959–), and the Committee of Ministers of the Council of Europe. Complaints were examined by the Commission and if declared admissible, the case was referred to the Court. If the case was not admissible, the Committee of Ministers decided whether there had been a violation of the Convention and, if appropriate, awarded "just satisfaction" to the victim. Protocol No. 11, which came into force on November 1, 1998, replaced the existing, part-time Court and Commission by a single, full-time Court.[10]

The ECHR has an excellent website containing basic texts, cases, annual reports, and other information. The case law is contained in a database called HUDOC.[11] This is the most comprehensive collection of decisions from the Commission and the

10. http://conventions.coe. int/.

11. http://cmiskp.echr.coe. int/tkp197/default.htm.

Court. You can search by words in the text of the decisions, treaty article, countries involved, and keyword. By using the keyword feature, you can search using a controlled vocabulary which will save you a lot of headaches since you won't be searching using the wrong terminology.

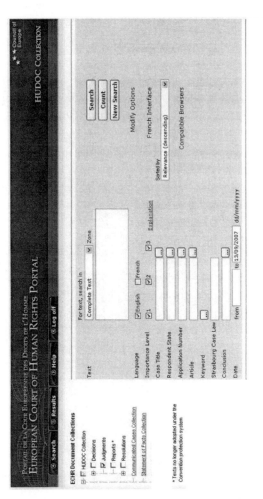

Figure 5: HUDOC Search

Another handy feature of this database is the "notice" attached to each case. A notice provides a nice rundown on the basics of the case, including information on the articles at issue, the case law cited, and any other relevant international law (see Figure 6).

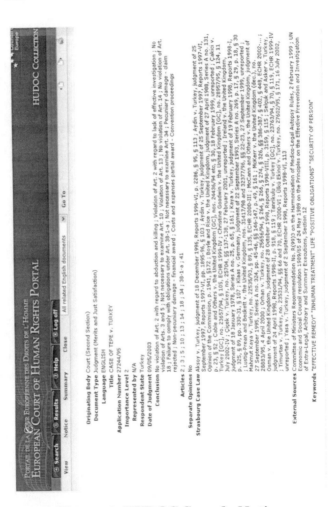

Figure 6: HUDOC Sample Notice

Besides the European system, there are two other human rights systems with formal dispute settlement mechanisms—the Inter–American system and the African system. While each of these has its own bodies of decisions, none are as active as the European system. There are also several quasi-judicial bodies in the UN human rights system. These bodies issue quite a bit of jurisprudence. For more details on researching this court and international human rights law, see Researching International Human Rights Law.[12]

E. Permanent Court of Arbitration (PCA)

This Court has evolved over the years to deal with disputes between States, intergovernmental organizations, and private parties in matters of both public and private international law. It was established by the Convention for the Pacific Settlement of International Disputes, concluded at The Hague in 1899 during the first Hague Peace Conference. The PCA website provides the text of founding and basic documents.[13] It also contains access to the treaties and agreements that refer to the PCA in the body of the text.

Article 63

Conciliation and arbitration proceedings may be held, if the parties so agree,

(a) at the seat of the Permanent Court of Arbitration or of any other appropriate institution, whether private or public, with which

---

12. http://www.law. berkeley.edu/library/online/ guides/international_foreign/ humanRights/index.html.

13. http://www.pca-cpa.org/ showpage.asp?pag_id=363.

the Centre may make arrangements for that purpose; or

(b) at any other place approved by the Commission or Tribunal after consultation with the Secretary–General.[14]

PCA decisions are available from a variety of print and electronic sources. Past and pending cases are available on its website and the PCA is working with the Hague Justice Portal to provide access to historic cases.[15] For more help with researching international arbitration, see the ASIL Guide to Electronic Sources for International Law: International Commercial Arbitration.[16]

There are other dispute settlement bodies in the area of arbitration. Two of the most prolific are the International Centre for Settlement of Investment Disputes (ICSID)[17] and the North American Free Trade Agreement (NAFTA).[18]

F. Other International Courts and Tribunals

There are several other international courts and tribunals, all of which issue decisions relevant for a

14. Convention on the Settlement of Investment Disputes between States and Nationals of Other States ("ICSID Convention"), March 18, 1965, 4 I.L.M. 524 (1965), art. 63.

15. http://www.hague Justiceportal.net/ecache/def/5/251.html.

16. http://www.asil.org/resource/arb1.htm.

17. http://www.worldbank.org/icsid/index.html.

18. http://www.naftaclaims.com/ and http://www.nafta-sec-alena.org/DefaultSite/index_e.aspx?DetailID=5.

variety of international research topics. Below we list them with relevant links provided.

- Inter–American Court of Human Rights[19]

- International Criminal Court[20]

- International Criminal Tribunals and Special Courts

  - International Criminal Tribunal for the Former Yugoslavia (ICTY)[21]

    Topical Digest of the Case Law (Human Rights Watch)[22]

  - International Criminal Tribunal for Rwanda (ICTR)[23]

  - Iraqi Special Tribunal

  - Extraordinary Chambers in the Courts of Cambodia (ECCC)[24]

    UN Assistance to the Khmer Rouge Trials (UNAKART)[25]

    Khmer Rouge Trial Task Force[26]

  - Special Court for Sierra Leone[27]

19.   http://www.corteidh.or.cr/.

20.   http://www.icc-cpi.int/home.html.

21.   http://www.un.org/icty/index.html.

22.   http://hrw.org/reports/2006/icty0706/.

23.   http://69.94.11.53/.

24.   http://www.eccc.gov.kh/english/default.aspx.

25.   http://www.unakrt-online.org/index.htm.

26.   http://www.cambodia.gov.kh/krt/english/index.htm.

27.   http://www.sc-sl.org/.

- International Tribunal for the Law of the Sea (ITLOS)[28]

- World Trade Organization, Dispute Settlement[29]

6.3 Other Useful Websites

The WorldLII International Courts & Tribunals Project is a website that provides searchable access to the decisions of many international courts and tribunals.[30] The website states that the site "aims to provide a comprehensive search facility for final decisions of all international and multi-national courts and tribunals, whether global or regional. The search facility below allows searches over the decisions of 20 International Courts and Tribunals, comprising over 20,000 decisions. Most databases contain complete backsets and are updated regularly."[31] This site can be searched as a whole or individual databases may be selected. Of course, the coverage offered for each court or tribunal varies.

28. http://www.itlos.org/

29. http://www.wto.org/ english/tratop_e/dispu_e/ dispu_e.htm

30. http://www.worldlii. org/int/cases/

31. http://www.worldlii. org/int/cases/

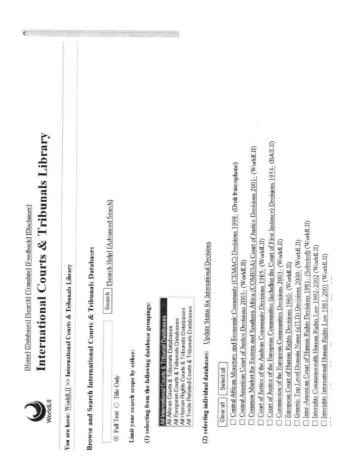

Figure 7: WorldLII Database

Other collections of case law exist on the web, such as the War Crimes Research Office (WCRO) Jurisprudence Collections.[32] This collection provides

32. https://www.wcl. american.edu/warcrimes/wcro_ docs/.

access to a series of collections of jurisprudence from various international courts and tribunals, such as the International Court of Justice and the Indonesian Human Rights Court. Some of the content is freely available and some requires registration and subscription. You can search or browse the collections.

As noted above, there is no one site that provides access to all of the decisions from international courts and tribunals. The same is true of print sources. The one print source that comes the closest is *International Law Reports* (1919–).[33] This publication contains full–text cases, translated into English, from both national and international tribunals. However, the coverage is selective and the translations take a while.

Recently, Oxford University Press launched a new database called International Law in Domestic Courts (ILDC).[34] ILDC is a collection of domestic cases that concern issues of international law from over 60 jurisdictions. The cases are selected by local reporters and feature expert commentary, full texts of judgments in their original language, and translations of key passages of non-English judgments into English.

Another mechanism for identifying relevant case law is through selective collections, such as M.

33. Previous titles were *Annual Digest of Public International Law Cases and Annual Digest* and *Reports of Public International Law Cases*.

34. http://ildc.oxfordlaw reports.com (by subscription).

Fitzmaurice, *Landmark Cases in Public International Law* (1998). Journal articles may also provide citations to relevant case law from a variety of international courts and tribunals.

Journal articles and books are quite helpful when you are trying to find cases on a specific topic. While most courts and tribunals have websites, their sites may not provide a user-friendly search mechanism or any other tool for locating cases by topic. This is when LexisNexis and Westlaw can provide more powerful search capabilities, but these databases do not provide access to all international courts, tribunals or quasi-judicial bodies. There is no one size fits all solution in this area.

To stay updated on new jurisprudence, there are a few tools available. ASIL and the International Judicial Academy produce one that is called *International Judicial Monitor*.[35] This free newsletter tracks judicial developments from around the world. Other similar tools include the *International Justice Tribunal*, an e-journal that covers international criminal justice and publishes investigative articles and interviews about world-wide efforts to try war criminals, from the International Criminal Court to domestic courts.[36] Since so many international courts are located in The Hague, the Hague Justice Portal[37] is a good place to get current information

35. http://www.judicial monitor.org/current/index. html.

36. http://www. justicetribune.com/ (by subscription).

37. http://www.hague justiceportal.net/.

and court documents from the following bodies: ICJ, ICC, ICTY, PCA, and the SCSL. This site also provides access to a good deal of research related to these bodies.

The writings of international tribunals are only going to grow in importance. The disorganized state in which they exist will continue to pose a challenge for the researcher, but the increasing availability of sources on the Internet and growing sophistication of the international bodies that produce the decisions will make life easier as time goes by.

CHAPTER 7

EUROPEAN UNION

7.1　Introduction

The European Union (EU) is a unique entity. Born of the dreams of cooperation that sprouted in post-World War II Europe, the EU is comprised of member countries that have surrendered a certain degree of sovereignty in exchange for the economic and political integration then made possible among the States. In theory, the system allows for countries to combine their resources. This allows certain political and economic policy decisions affecting Europe to be made collectively. The EU system allows for the adoption of common policies involving issues that include agriculture, consumer affairs, culture, the environment, energy, transportation, and trade.

The EU evolved on the premise that collaboration among European nations could put an end to irreconcilable conflicts and generate a more efficient and beneficial system for making policy decisions amicably. Though it has its faults it is important to recognize that the EU represents a real achievement. The authors of this Nutshell recall when many doubted that it could be done at all. It is important to remember that the EU is not meant to create one entity that replaces existing European States. These member countries maintain a significant amount of sovereignty. Today, the EU's greatest challenge is fostering continued economic and political integration among its members while member countries continue to employ their sovereignty in making independent decisions.

7.2   The Formation of the EU

The origins of European integration can be traced to the series of bloody conflicts between France and Germany from 1870–1945, which some economists and historians have ascribed to a struggle over production of raw materials. In 1950, in the context of a war weary Europe, French Foreign Minister Robert Schuman urged France and Germany to institute a common Higher Authority to regulate the overall production of coal and steel. It was Schuman that proposed, "the pooling of coal and steel production [would] immediately provide for the setting up of common foundations for economic development and as a first step in the federation of Europe."[1] This idea sparked the creation of the European Coal and Steel Community (ECSC) in 1951, made up of six members: Belgium, West Germany, Luxembourg, France, Italy, and the Netherlands. The High Authority proposed in the Schuman Plan served as an independent body charged with making all coal and steel industry decisions involving these countries.

In 1957, after the celebrated success of the ECSC, the original six member states drafted and signed two treaties that were integral to the formation of the EU. They are known as the "Treaties of Rome." The first of the two treaties was originally called the Treaty Establishing the European Eco-

1. Schuman Declaration, May 9, 1950, http://europa.eu/ abc/symbols/9–may/decl_en. htm.

nomic Community (EC Treaty).[2] The second treaty is called the European Atomic Energy Committee (Euratom Treaty). Together, these treaties were intended to remove trade barriers among these member countries and provide guidelines for the formation of a common market. In 1967, the EC replaced its existing institutions with a European Commission, Council of Ministers, and Parliament.

The structural changes in 1967 preface a series of treaties that better define today's EU's structural organization. The Treaty of Maastricht (formerly the Treaty on European Union) created what we refer to today as the European Union, a single currency for the EU, and the EU's three-pillar system. This treaty also introduced new methods of cooperation among the governments of member states especially in the areas of defense and home affairs.

The Treaty of Maastricht was further supplemented by the Treaty of Amsterdam in 1997 and the Treaty of Nice in 2001. Both of these treaties were designed to handle the challenges resulting from the burgeoning membership of the European Union. To ensure that the expanding EU could continue functioning efficiently, a more streamlined system for decision-making was an absolute necessity. The Treaty of Nice introduced new rules governing the size of the EU institutions and the functions they serve. If approved by all EU member states, an official EU Constitution was scheduled for ratifica-

2. In 1992, the Maastricht Treaty amended the EC Treaty and removed the word "economic" from its title.

tion in 2006. However, due to some ratification problems, the EU entered into a "period of reflection," and in June 2007, decided not to pass a Constitution. Instead, an Intergovernmental Conference (IGC) was convened to work on drafting a reform treaty and the Treaty of Lisbon was signed on December 13, 2007.[3] This treaty amends the current EU and EC treaties and the target date for ratification is January 1, 2009.[4]

7.3 The EU Today

The EU's membership now totals 27 countries including Austria, Belgium, Cyprus, the Czech Republic, Denmark, Estonia, Finland, France, Germany, Greece, Hungary, Ireland, Italy, Latvia, Lithuania, Luxembourg, Malta, the Netherlands, Poland, Portugal, Slovakia, Slovenia, Sweden, Spain, and the United Kingdom. Other countries wish to join the EU, and issues of admitting new members are not without complications

7.4 The Euro

As a symbol of a single European market, the euro represents one of the most significant economic reforms in history and serves as the official currency of the EU. Even non-EU states of Europe including Monaco and the Vatican City have adopted the euro as their currency. The European System of Central Banks administers the euro and

3. http://europa.eu/reform_treaty/index_en.htm.

4. http://europa.eu/lisbon_treaty/take/index_en.htm.

possesses sole authority to set the EU's monetary policy. The United Kingdom has not adopted the euro.

7.5   The Three Pillars of the EU

The EU's three-pillar structure is a way of categorizing its three main policy areas. The three pillars are: 1) the Community pillar, 2) the Common Foreign and Security Policy (CFSP) pillar, and 3) the Justice and Home Affairs pillar. The Community pillar manages social, economic and environmental policies on issues including the trade of goods, services and monetary policy. The Common Foreign and Security Policy (CFSP) pillar is charged with creating integrated EU policies on military matters and foreign affairs. Many members want to retain sovereignty in this area, which has presented a genuine challenge to the CFSP's mission. The Justice and Home Affairs pillar manages police and judicial cooperation in criminal matters including drug trafficking and terrorism. The Community pillar is the only pillar where decisions can be made with concurrence by a majority of Member States. The other two pillars require unanimity for decisions to be passed.

7.6   The EU's Organizational Structure

The governmental structure of the EU is divided among five institutions that create a system of checks and balances: the European Commission,

European Parliament, the Council of the European Union, The European Court of Justice, and the European Court of Auditors.[5] Each of these institutions has a specific role in the shaping, implementation, and monitoring of policy and regulations devised by the EU.

A. The European Commission, http://ec. europa.eu/index_en.htm

Based in Brussels, the European Commission serves as the executive branch of the EU, managing policies and the annual budget. The EC is responsible for drafting all legislative and policy proposals for European laws. These proposals are then submitted to the Council and to the European Parliament for amendment and approval.

After consultation with the European Parliament, the President of the Commission is nominated by common agreement among the governments of the member states. The nomination of the President is accompanied by the nomination of 27 Commissioners. Commissioners are nominated by the governments of each member state according to its own selection procedure. The Parliament must then vote to approve the appointment of the President and the other members of the Commission. If the appointment of any Commissioner is denied by the Parliament, the selection process must start again.

The President of the Commission determines what area of policy will be managed by each Com-

5. See   http://europa.eu/ institutions/index_en.htm.

missioner. These policy areas are generally referred to as portfolios. Commissioners are not allowed to be assigned a portfolio that would involve the interests of the member state they represent. They are expected to act independently and in the best interest of the EU as a whole. Each Commissioner may select a cabinet consisting of approximately five counselors who assist in the preparation of Commission decisions.

B. The European Parliament, http://www.europarl.europa.eu/news/public/default_en.htm?redirection

The European Parliament, a legislative body elected by universal suffrage, monitors the European Commission and is charged with overseeing the EU budget. Although the Parliament's official headquarters are located in Strasbourg, the majority of its committee work and plenary sessions take place in Brussels. The 732 members of the European Parliament (MEPs) are not organized by nationality, but by political allegiance. The next parliament will be elected in 2009 when the five-year cycle of the previous one ends.

C. The Council of the European Union, http://www.consilium.europa.eu/

The European Parliament shares its legislative power with the Council of the European Union (also known as the Council of Ministers), the main decision making body of the EU. Presidency of the

Council is held for six months by each member state on a rotational basis. The Council serves as a forum for the government ministers representing EU member states.

D.   The European Court of Justice, http://curia.europa.eu/en/transitpage.htm

Sitting in Luxembourg, the European Court of Justice serves as the judicial organ of the European Community. Each of the Member States appoints a judge to serve on the Court to ensure that all legal systems of member countries are represented. Of the Court's delegated duties, one of its primary functions is to ensure that Community law is applied throughout the member states. The Court can settle legal disputes between EU member states, EU institutions, businesses and individuals.

E.   The   Court   of   Auditors,   http://eca.europa.eu/portal/page/portal/eca_main_pages/home

Also based in Luxembourg, the Court of Auditors was set up in 1975 as an ancillary body for monitoring the EU budget. The Court consists of one member from each country belonging to the EU who is appointed by the Council for a term of six years. The Court "checks that all the European Union's revenue has been received and all its expenditure incurred in a lawful and regular manner and that the EU budget has been managed soundly."[6]

6.   http://europa.eu/abc/12 lessons/index4_en.htm.

F.　Additional EU Bodies, http://europa.eu/ institutions/index_en.htm

There are additional entities that work in collaboration with the five main institutions of the EU: the European Economic and Social Committee, the Committee of the Regions, the European Central Bank, the European Ombudsman, and the European Investment Bank.

The European Economic and Social Committee (EESC) is an advisory body representing employers, trade unions, farmers, consumers and other interest groups. The EESC serves as a representative for these interest groups and presents their concerns during policy discussions with the Commission, the Council and the European Parliament.

The Committee of the Regions (CoR) is comprised of representatives of Europe's regional and local authorities. According to the Treaty on European Union, the CoR must be consulted before the EU can make decisions on matters that concern local and regional governments.[7]

Also set up under the Treaty of the European Union, the European Central Bank is responsible for instituting the EU's monetary policy and managing the euro. The European Investment Bank (EIB) was created under the Treaty of Rome. As a non-profit entity, the EIB uses separate funds from the EU budget to invest in countries who are candidates for membership to the EU, small businesses,

7.　Treaty on European Union, Feb. 7, 1992, 1992 O.J. (C191) 1, 31 I.L.M. 253 (1992).

and developing nations at large. The money serves as an investment tool for international development and progress.

The European Ombudsman is elected for a five-year term and is charged with serving as an intermediary between citizens and EU authorities. When citizens, businesses, organizations, and anyone else that has a registered office in an EU country want to file grievances, it is the Ombudsman who receives and investigates them.

7.7 European Union Documents

The EU document system is as massive as the U.N. system. But there is good news: the EU has taken full advantage of the web as a mechanism for distributing documents. But before going straight to the computer to search for documents, an overview of the documentation available from EU bodies and institutions is in order.

For most researchers, EUROPA,[8] the official website of the European Union, is the best place to start since it provides a tremendous amount of the most important documentation and information. Launched in 1995, "[t]he aim of EUROPA is to act as a portal for access to all the institutions of the European Union and to the activities carried out by them in accordance with the powers vested in them under the Treaties."[9] This website is actually a

8. http://europa.eu.int/.   9.   http://europa.eu.int/
abouteuropa/faq/q02/index_en.
htm.

collection of numerous databases which provides access to information and documentation from the institutions and bodies of the European Union, including the European Parliament, the Council of the Union, the Commission, the Court of Justice, the Court of Auditors, the Economic and Social Committee, the Committee of the Regions, the European Central Bank and the European Investment Bank. For the most part, this portal is available in all of the 23 official languages of the EU, and there is no charge to access any of the documents.

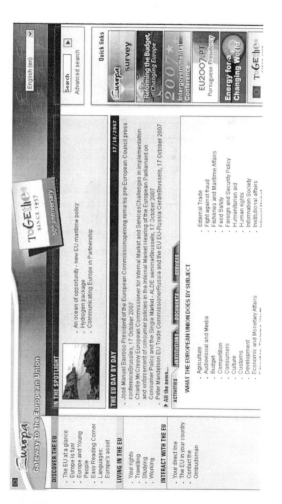

Figure 1: EUROPA Homepage

Of particular importance to the legal researcher is EUR–Lex, the "portal to European Union Law."[10]

10. http://eur-lex.eu ropa.eu.

This version of EUR–Lex is the result of a merger between the old site with the CELEX database. This should be the first database consulted by the legal researcher since it contains a variety of documents: treaties, international agreements, legislation in force, legislation in preparation, case law, and parliamentary questions. Like other parts of EUROPA, access to this collection of documents is also free.

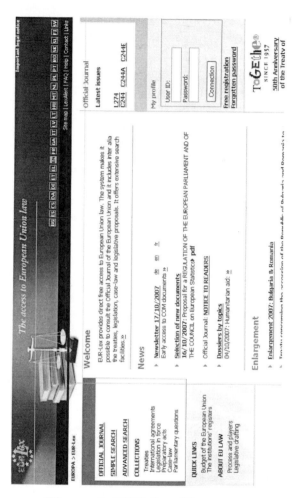

Figure 2: EUR–Lex Homepage

Be aware of eurojargon. Sometimes you may need to consult a glossary for help with definitions of unfamiliar terminology.[11] See also *Eurojargon: A Dictionary of European Union Acronyms, Abbreviations and Terminology* (7th ed. 2004).

7.8 Some Basics for Doing EU Legal Research

The *Official Journal of the European Communities* (often cited to as OJ) is divided into two series. The *L Series* contains adopted treaties and legislation, including directives and regulations, adopted by the Commission and Council, and other founding acts. The *C Series* is the "Information and Notices" section of the OJ containing non-binding decisions and resolutions of the institutions, texts of proposed legislation, minutes of the Parliament, Commission and Council replies to written questions, opinions of the Economic and Social Committee, and notices of Court decisions. While much of the OJ is available on EUROPA, not all issues are necessarily accessible. The OJ can be browsed from 1998 to present[12] and others years can be searched for by citation or date.[13]

11. http://europa.eu/ scadplus/glossary/index_en. htm.

12. http://europa.eu.int/ eur-lex/lex/JOIndex.do? ihmlang=en.

13. http://europa.eu.int/ eur-lex/lex/RECH_reference_ pub.do.

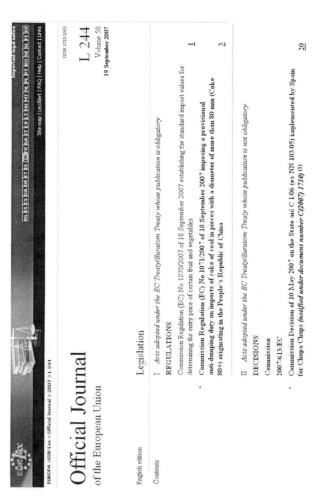

Figure 3: Official Journal L Series

Site map | Lex-alert | FAQ | Help | Contact | Links

Important legal notice

BG ES CS DA DE ET EL EN FR GA IT LV LT HU MT NL PL PT RO SK SL FI SV

ISSN 1725-2423

Official Journal
of the European Union

C 219

Volume 50

19 September 2007

English edition

Information and Notices

Notice No	Contents	page
	II *Information*	
	INFORMATION FROM EUROPEAN UNION INSTITUTIONS AND BODIES	
	Commission	
2007/C 219/01	Amendments to the Explanatory Note to Article 17 of the pan-Euro-Mediterranean protocols on rules of origin	1
2007/C 219/02	Non-opposition to a notified concentration (Case COMP/M.4780 — WL Ross/C&A Automotive Interior Businesses) (1)	2
	IV *Notices*	
	NOTICES FROM EUROPEAN UNION INSTITUTIONS AND BODIES	
	Commission	
2007/C 219/03	Euro exchange rates	3

Figure 4: Official Journal C Series

7.9 Legislation

A. European Union Treaties

The basic legal texts upon which the European
Union and the European Communities are based
are the treaties: the founding treaties, plus amendments; the accession treaties for each of the five
enlargements; and other important documents.[14]
While these treaties are available on many websites,
EUROPA provides the text in html, pdf and tiff
format. The version of the treaty from the Official
Journal is available in pdf. Treaties are also available in print and on LexisNexis and Westlaw.

Primary legislation includes the founding (or
constitutive) treaties from the ESCS Treaty of 1957
to the Treaty of Nice of 2001. A second source of
primary law consists of the treaties between Member States and treaties between the EU and third
parties.

B. Secondary Legislation

The major source of Community legislation is
secondary legislation: regulations, directives, and
decisions. A few definitions are in order.

* Regulations are Community laws adopted by
  the Council of the European Union upon a
  proposal from the Commission. Regulations
  have general effect and are directly applicable

14. http://europa.eu.int/   htm.
eur-lex/lex/en/treaties/index.

in all of the Member States. Regulations do not require national implementing legislation.

- Directives are Community laws adopted by the Council of the European Union upon a proposal from the Commission. Directives are addressed to the Member States and are binding as to the result—Member States may choose the form and methods of implementation. The process of implementation is called harmonization.

- Decisions are Community laws, issued by the Council or Commission, which are binding on those addressed, whether they be governments, companies or individuals.

- Opinions are written statements by the Council or Commission and have no binding force. Opinions are an important indication of Council or Commission policy.

- Recommendations adopted by the Commission are like directives in that they are applicable only on the Member States cited and only with respect to the end result. They have no binding force.

7.10 Documentation of EU Institutions

Each EU institution (outlined in section 7.6) generates specific documents and reports. The aim here is to focus on the documents of most interest to a legal researcher. For access and explanation of other documents, see the EUROPA website, under the "Documents" tab.[15]

One of the most important institutions in the legal area is the European Commission[16] since it has both executive and administrative roles. The Commission is organized into departments, called Directorate Generals, responsible for drafting legislation and overseeing its implementation. In its executive capacity, the Commission acts as the "government" in a Parliamentary system by initiating legislation and submitting proposals to the Council of the European Union. The Commission also oversees Member States' implementation of directives and enforces regulations.

Commission documents (also known as COM documents) are good for explanatory memorandum and the text of proposed legislation. The Commission also produces Green and White Papers and SEC documents. Green papers are discussion papers published by the Commission on a specific policy area. White papers are documents containing proposals for Community action in a specific area. SEC documents are internal documents associated with the decision-making process and the general operation of Commission departments. The Commission's website makes many of these documents available, some even before the 1990s.

The Council of the European Union[17] (also known as the Council of Ministers) is the main decision-

15.   http://europa.eu/index_
en.htm.

16.   http://europa.eu.int/
comm/index_en.htm.

17.   http://www.consilium.
europa.eu/showPage.ASP?
lang=en.

making body of the EU. It represents the Member States, acts on Commission proposals, and has the final legislative authority. The Council may request that certain legislation be proposed and may conduct any necessary studies to help achieve the goals of foundational treaties. The Council also has treaty-making power.

The Council issues working papers on legislation, minutes and other documents. See the "Documents"[18] section of the website for access to these documents, organized into a variety of sectors, such as Community policies, European and Monetary Union, and Access to Council Documents (public register). A recent addition to this site is the Agreements database[19] which includes agreements with third countries as well as other international organizations. If the treaty has been published in the Official Journal, a link to the OJ will be available from this database.

The European Parliament[20] is composed of Representatives directly elected by the populations of the Member States. In most cases, the Council is required to submit proposed legislation to the European Parliament for comment. The Parliament acts as a forum for debate and for the questioning of the Council and Commission. The appropriate commit-

18. http://www.consilium. europa.eu/docCenter.asp? lang=en & cmsid=245.

19. http://www.consilium. europa.eu/cms3_applications/ Applications/accords/search. asp?lang=EN & cmsID=297.

20. http://www.europarl. europa.eu/news/public/default_ en.htm.

tee of the Parliament scrutinizes the proposed legislation and a rapporteur is selected to draft a report and opinion for consideration at the plenary meeting. The Parliament adopts legislation "in codecision"[21] with the Commission.

For first or second readings of Commission proposals, see Reports, which generally consists of three parts: 1) record of the Committee's action, 2) explanatory memorandum providing background on an issue and reasons for the Committee's recommendation, and 3) text of the draft opinion. Minutes of plenary session considering the rapporteur's report are printed in the C series of the OJ. Debates of the plenary sessions of Parliament are in the Annex of the OJ. Other documents are available under the "Activities" section of the Parliament's website.[22]

The Economic and Social Committee[23] is an advisory body representing industry, labor and consumers, and is composed of members appointed by the Member States. During the legislative process, the Council of Ministers may be required or may on its own initiative decide to seek the opinion of the Committee.

21. "The codecision procedure (Article 251 of the EC Treaty) was introduced by the Treaty of Maastricht. It gives the European Parliament the power to adopt instruments jointly with the Council of the European Union." See http://europa.eu.int/scadplus/glossary/codecision_procedure_en.htm for more information.

22. http://www.europarl.europa.eu/activities/public.do?language=en.

23. http://eesc.europa.eu/index_en.asp.

Documents and texts from the Economic and Social Committee are available in the C series of the OJ and on Committee's website (under "Documents").

The European Court of Justice[24] is the highest legal authority in the EU. The Court is empowered to decide cases involving interpretation and application of the Treaties. EU institutions and Member States may appeal and take each other to court for failure to implement or properly apply the Treaties and derived legislation (for example, the Commission will file a case against a Member State for not implementing a directive). Legal or natural persons may appeal to the Court against a decision addressed to him or any regulation or decision which is of direct concern. The Court will also issue prejudicial decisions in cases referred to it by national courts when questions of Community law are involved. The Court is assisted by advocate-generals, who present a reasoned and independent opinion of the issue of law in the case. While there is no formal doctrine of stare decisis, the Court tends to follow its own decisions. The decisions are binding on the national courts of Member States.

In 1989, the Court of First Instance began functioning, hearing disputes between community civil servants and their institutions, actions in the field of competition law, actions under anti-dumping law and actions under the ECSC Treaty. There is also a

24. http://curia.eu.int/en/ index.htm.

European Court of Auditors that is responsible for checking on the management of the EU budget.[25]

The judgments from both courts are available in the official *European Court Reports* series (ECR), the Court's website, and LexisNexis and Westlaw.

7.11 Finding Directives & Regulations

All directives and regulations are published in the "L" series of the OJ and EUR–Lex is the best place to obtain legislation. If you have the OJ citation, use EUR–Lex as noted below. Otherwise, there is a simple and an advanced search tool on the site. Save yourself some headaches and use the simple search since it is pretty powerful and allows you to search by a variety of search terms.

Take this citation: Council regulation (EC) 1236/2005, 2005 OJ L 200/1.

If you have the OJ citations, as noted above, you can go directly to the Official Journal and get what you need. The OJ is available on EUR–Lex, print, LexisNexis and Westlaw (as well as a few other databases). If you only have the numbers for the EU legislation (1236/2005 or 2001/20/EC) and not a clue where to go, start with EUR–Lex. For example, search 1236/2005 on EUR–Lex, by selecting the simple search (Figure 5); search by document number (select "natural number"); type in the year and

25. http://eca.europa.eu/ portal/page/portal/eca_main_ pages/home.

number in the appropriate boxes (Figure 6); and you will retrieve two results (Figure 7).

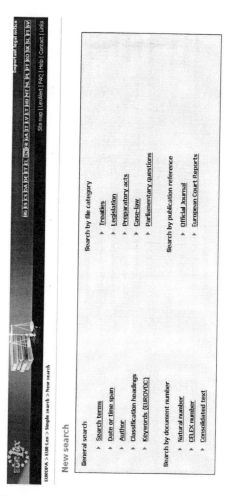

Figure 5: EUR–Lex Simple Search

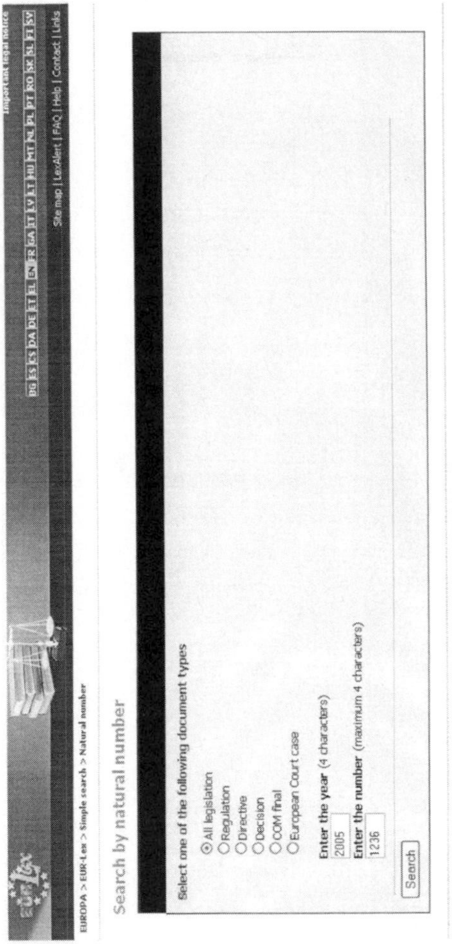

Figure 6: EUR–Lex Natural Number Search

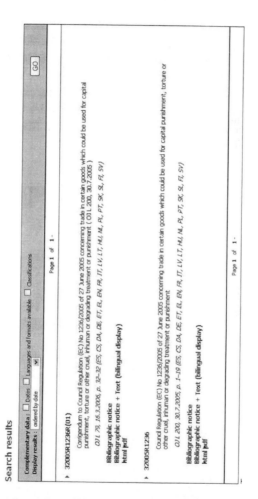

Figure 7: EUR–Lex Search Results

One the most useful aspects of EUR–Lex is the "bibliographic notice" listed under each result. This bibliographic notice document is amazing. From here, you can get the text of the legislation, learn about the proper classifications (using Euro-jargon), get a COM document number (the Commission's proposal for the legislation), find the legal basis from the founding treaties, amendments, citations to case law from the European Court of Justice, and more–all for free!

Of course, you won't always have a citation to the piece of legislation. Say you need a directive on the conduct of clinical trials on medicine for human use. Using the same simple search mechanism used above, search first by "Category" and search by "Legislation" instead of by "Document Number" as done above (see Figure 8); select "Search Option" using "Search Terms" (Figure 9); and search using the terms "clinical trials" (Figure 10). This search retrieves one result and you can also utilize the detailed "bibliographic notice" as mentioned above or go directly to the document (Figure 11).

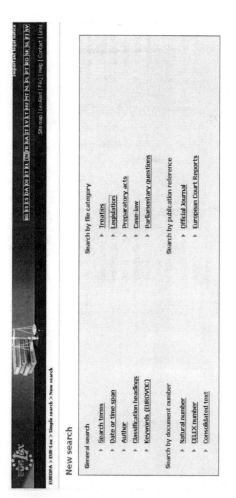

Figure 8: EUR–Lex Simple Search for Legislation

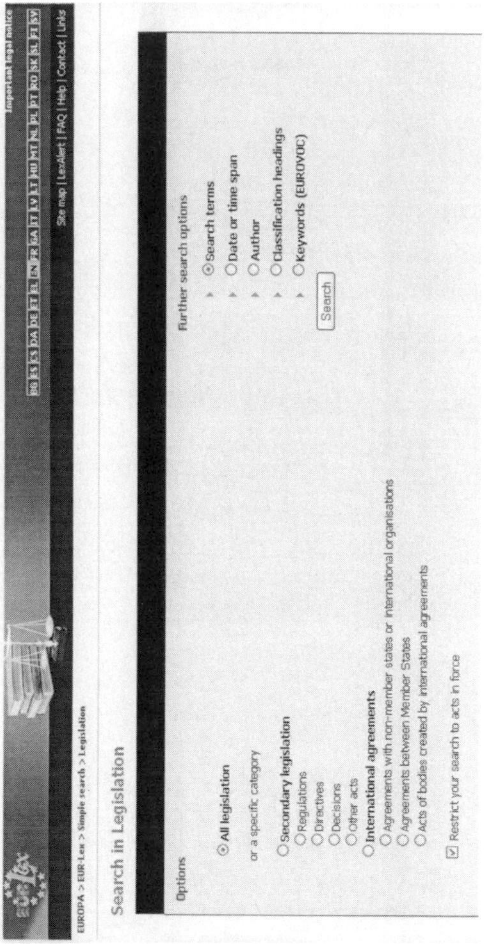

Figure 9: EUR–Lex Search Terms Option

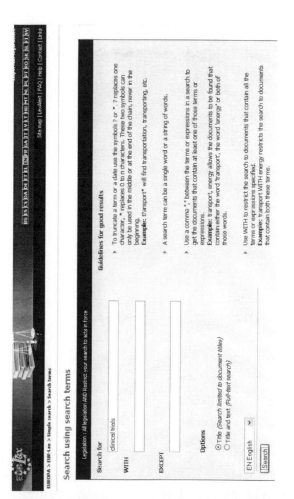

Figure 10: EUR–Lex Search Using Search Terms

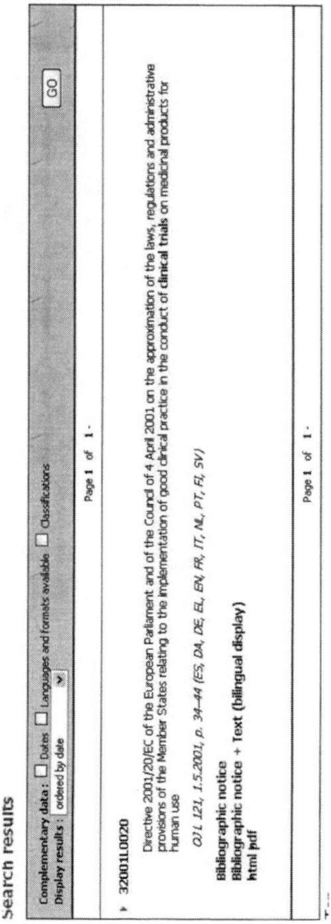

Search results

Complementary data : ☐ Dates ☐ Languages and formats available ☐ Classifications
Display results : ordered by date ▾

Page **1** of **1** ·

▸ **32001L0020**

Directive 2001/20/EC of the European Parliament and of the Council of 4 April 2001 on the approximation of the laws, regulations and administrative provisions of the Member States relating to the implementation of good clinical practice in the conduct of **clinical trials** on medicinal products for human use

OJ L 121, 1.5.2001, p. 34–44 (ES, DA, DE, EL, EN, FR, IT, NL, PT, FI, SV)

Bibliographic notice
Bibliographic notice + Text (bilingual display)
html pdf

Page **1** of **1** ·

GO

Figure 11: EUR–Lex Search Results

7.12   Implementing Legislation

Directives require that Member States implement them by passing national legislation. Locating implementing legislation is not as easy as locating the EU directive. The EUR–Lex "bibliographic notice" has a section at the bottom of the record labeled "Display the national implementing measures" (Figures 12 and 13). While no legislation is linked to the record, at least you have information to use to locate the text of the document.

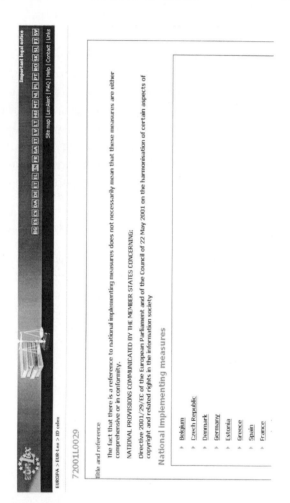

Figure 12: National Implementing Measures

Belgium:

1. - Loi du 22 mai 2005 transposant en droit belge la Directive 2001/29/CE du 22 mai 2001 sur l'harmonisation de certains aspects du droit d'auteur et des droits voisins dans la société de l'information

Czech Republic:

1. - Zákon o právu autorském, o právech souvisejících s právem autorským a o změně některých zákonů (autorský zákon)

2. - Zákon č. 140/1961 Sb., trestní zákon

3. - Zákon České národní rady č. 200/1990 Sb., o přestupcích

4. - Zákon č. 81/2005 Sb., kterým se mění zákon č. 121/2000 Sb., o právu autorském, o právech souvisejících s právem autorským a o změně některých zákonů (autorský zákon)

Denmark:

1. - Lov om aendring af ophavsretsloven ref: Lov nº 1051 du 17/12/2002 p. 7881

Germany:

1. - Gesetz zur Regelung des Urheberrechts in der Informationsgesellschaft vom 10/09/2003 BGBl. Teil I nº 46 vom 12/09/2003 p. 1774

Estonia:

1. - Autoriõiguse seadus

Greece:

1. - Acte législatif nº 3057/2002 FEK A nº 239 du 10/10/2002 p. 4555

Spain:

NO REFERENCE AVAILABLE

France:

NO REFERENCE AVAILABLE

Figure 13: List of National Legislation

LexisNexis and Westlaw also provide references to national legislation. On LexisNexis, these references are listed at the end of the document, while Westlaw lists the "national measures" by Member

States at the end of the document, usually in the language of the country.

An experimental website is available called N–Lex—"a common gateway to national law."[26] This site does not provide access to national law, but it does allow you to search national legislative databases in a standard way, more or less.[27] The laws are not translated into English, unless English is one of the official languages for that country. There is a "general introduction" to the legislative database for each country and this is often in English. By consulting the "national implementing measures" section of EUR–Lex, you can identify the needed legislation and then use N–Lex to obtain the law. For example, look at the Copyright Directive from Figures 12 and 13 above. Note that in Belgium a law was passed in 2005 to implement that directive. Using the information from EUR–Lex, you can search N–Lex to obtain the full-text of the law.

Belgium:

1.—Loi du 22 mai 2005 transposant en droit belge la Directive 2001/29/CE du 22 mai 2001 sur l'harmonisation de certains aspects du droit d'auteur et des droits voisins dans la société de l'information.

Search N–Lex using the search form for the Belgium consolidated legislation, Moniteur (in French or Dutch) (see Figure 14). This retrieves one result (see Figure 15) and you can access the complete text

26. http://eur-lex.europa. eu/n-lex/.

27. http://www.eia.org.uk/ database_natimp1.htm.

of the law in French (see Figure 16). While this is rather like trying to explain to someone how to ride a bicycle, trust us it works. Give it a try.

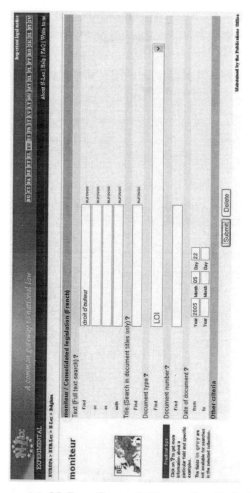

Figure 14: N–Lex Search Form for Belgium

Figure 15: N–Lex Search results

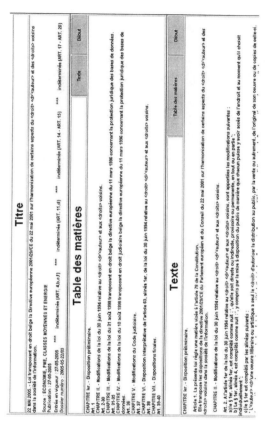

Figure 16: Full–Text of Belgian Law

See Chapter 3 of this Nutshell for help with researching foreign law.

7.13   Case Law

There are many tools available for locating the jurisprudence of the European Court of Justice. Using the EUR–Lex simple search is one way. In addition, the Court has its own website called Curia.[28] On this site, you can search by completing a search form (see Figure 17), browsing a numerical

28.   http://curia.europa.eu/
en/index.htm.

list, or using a digest and alphabetical list—if you can read French.

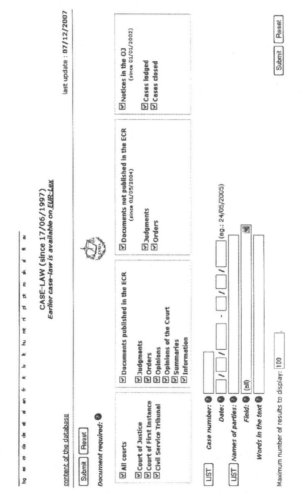

Figure 17: Case law Search Form

7.14　Background Sources

Launching into an analysis of European Union law through legislation can be overwhelming. Since there are many good books published on the EU and on any number of topics, a quick review of these sources is worth the time.

Encyclopedia of European Union Law (1996–).

Ralph Folsom, *European Union Law in a Nutshell* (5th ed. 2005).

Trevor C. Hartley, *The Foundations of European Community Law: An Introduction to the Constitutional and Administrative Law of the European Community* (6th ed. 2007).

P.S.R.F. Mathijsen, *A Guide to European Union Law* (9th ed. 2007).

Rudden and Wyatt's EU Treaties and Legislation (9th ed. 2004).

Wyatt and Dashwood's European Union Law (5th ed. 2006).

7.15　Other Useful Tools

Many helpful folks have posted other tools and guides on the web which will help the novice or the experienced EU law researcher. Here is a short list:

European Union A to Z Index[29]
Prepared by the Delegation to the European Commission to the USA, this is a handy guide to websites by topics and bodies.

Essential European Union Law Websites[30]
Prepared by the Delegation to the European Commission to the USA listing key websites for EU law.

European Union Law: An Integrated Guide to Electronic and Print Research[31]

European Union Legal Materials: An Infrequent User's Guide[32]

LAWLINKS: European Union[33]

29. http://www.eurunion. org/infores/euindex.htm.

30. http://www.eurunion. org/infores/BestLawSites. HTM.

31. http://www.llrx.com/ features/eulaw2.htm.

32. http://www. nyulawglobal.com/globalex/ European_Union.htm.

33. http://www.kent.ac.uk/ lawlinks/eurounion.html.

CHAPTER 8

UNITED NATIONS

8.1 Introduction

As the world's largest and most inclusive global organization, the United Nations gives rise to a wide range of misconceptions regarding its structure and purpose. From the idea that it functions as a world government policing international affairs, to the notion that it is a mere toothless bureaucracy devoid of meaningful influence—the U.N. is widely scrutinized. A more apt description, however, is that the U.N. plays an important, though evolving, diplomatic role in an increasingly complex global setting. Although the United Nations is not a world government, and it does not pass laws in the traditional sense, it does provide a framework and forum for resolving international conflicts and developing foreign policy. As such, it generates a veritable avalanche of documents in every possible format. An overview of the U.N.'s formation and a summary of its six primary bodies offers a basic understanding of the U.N.'s role in international affairs. It will assist researchers in battling the most common misconceptions and perhaps make research that touches on U.N. materials a bit less mysterious.

8.2 The League of Nations: Predecessor to the United Nations

While the history of international efforts to create a global peacekeeping body is quite vast, the seminal event is the founding of the League of Nations following the end of the First World War. As part of an agreement between Germany and the Allies to end the global conflict, the League of Nations was established under the Treaty of Versailles "to promote international cooperation and to achieve peace and security."[1] The League of Nations was an association of states that pledged not to go to war before submitting their disputes to formal arbitration or inquiry. This mechanism was designed to prevent acts of unilateral aggression and to promote a more stable geopolitical system.

The League of Nations formally came into existence on January 10, 1920. Autonomous but closely connected to the League of Nations were the Permanent Court of International Justice and the International Labor Organization. The League also established subsidiary bodies to promote cooperation on economic, social, health, and intellectual matters. Lacking formal support and participation from the United States, the League of Nations never achieved strong influence globally. After failing to prevent the Second World War, the League ceased its activities. When the Second World War ended, the demise of the League of Nations and a global desire for peace prompted the need for a similar organization to carry the torch—the result was the creation of the United Nations.

8.3   The Formation of the United Nations

The need for an international organization to replace the League of Nations was first acknowledged during World War II, in the Moscow Declara-

1. The Versailles Treaty, June 28, 1919.

tion issued by China, Great Britain, the United States, and the USSR on October 30, 1943.[2] Following the end of the war in 1945, representatives of 50 nations attended the founding conference in San Francisco, where they drafted and later signed the U.N. charter.[3] The required 29 nations ratified the charter on October 26, 1945, making the organization official.

The current membership of the United Nations totals 192 countries. Agreement and acceptance of the obligations put forth in the U.N. Charter are required for a State to become a member of the U.N. A defining feature of U.N. membership remains the fact that Member States relinquish none of their sovereignty in exchange for membership. The Charter is designed as an international treaty outlining the basic principles of international relations. According to the Charter, the U.N. has four purposes: (1) to maintain international peace and security; (2) to develop friendly relations among nations; (3) to cooperate in solving international problems and in promoting respect for human rights; and (4) to be a center for harmonizing the actions of nations.[4]

2. In addition to proposing the need for an international organization for peace, the Moscow Declaration demanded the unconditional surrender of the Axis powers and declared Germany's annexation of Austria illegal.

3. L.M. Goodrich et al., *Charter of the United Nations: Commentary and Documents*, (3d ed. 1969).

4. U.N. Charter art. 1, paras. 1–4.

8.4   A Roadmap: The Organizational Structure of the U.N.

Like any complex political system, the United Nations consists of several branches that have specific powers and responsibilities. In fact, given its organization and its name, it is no surprise that the U.N. has been confused for a world government. Of its six main entities, five of them are based at U.N. Headquarters in New York: the Security Council, the Secretariat, the General Assembly, the Economic and Social Council, and the Trusteeship Council. The sixth, the International Court of Justice, is located at The Hague in the Netherlands.

A. The Security Council, http://www.un.org/Docs/sc/

The Security Council's primary role is to lead U.N. decision-making with regard to threats against international peace and acts of aggression.[5] The Council also acts as part of the broader U.N. leadership in advising the decision making of the General Assembly in such matters as choosing a new Secretary General or admitting new Member States. Under the U.N. Charter, all members are obligated to abide by the Council's decisions.

Of the 15 Council members, five nations have permanent seats: China, France, the Russian Federation, the United Kingdom and the United States. The other 10 are elected by the General Assembly

5. U.N. Charter, ch. VII, art. 39.

for two-year terms. Nine affirmative votes are required in order for decisions by the Council to be passed. Each of the five permanent members has veto power. This means that any one of the five permanent members can stop any decision from being made. The only exception to this rule is when procedural matters are under consideration.

The Security Council may meet at any time. If the Council determines a situation to be a potential threat to international peace, it will convene and initiate an attempt to mediate and resolve the conflict peacefully. If a conflict has already resulted in an attack, the Council will make haste towards reaching a ceasefire. The Council has the authority to assign peacekeeping missions in those situations where parties require more assistance in maintaining truces or where a physical separation of opposing forces is imperative. These are often matters of great sensitivity.

The Security Council is unique among the U.N. bodies in that it has the capacity to enact coercive measures for enforcing its decisions. Enforcement measures include the imposition of economic sanctions or orders for arms embargos.[6] Under extreme circumstances, the Council has authorized Member States to use "all necessary means," including the use of military force by Member States.[7] For exam-

---

6. U.N. Charter art. 40.

7. S.C. Res. 687, U.N. Doc. S/RES/687 (1991). In March 1991, the concluding month of Operation Desert Storm, the terms of ceasefire were drafted. Saddam Hussein consented to the United Nations Security Council Resolution 687. The resolution required Iraq to end

ple, the Council used this authority to give Member States the green light to invade Iraq during the Gulf War in 1990.

B. The Secretariat, http://www.un.org/documents/st.htm

The substantive and administrative work of the United Nations is managed by the Secretariat under the direction of the General Assembly, the Security Council and other U.N. entities. The Secretariat is headed by the Secretary–General[8] and currently requires a total staff of almost 8,900 that operate under both the general budget and special funding. Staff members represent approximately 170 countries located at duty stations that range from U.N. Headquarters in New York City to U.N. offices abroad including Geneva, Vienna, and Nairobi.

C. The General Assembly, http://www.un.org/ga/

All U.N. Member States are represented in the General Assembly, a "parliament of nations," which meets to grapple with the world's most pressing problems. All Member States share equal participation in these affairs and each is allowed one vote. A two-thirds majority is required for all decisions that involve international peace and security, the

its weapons of mass destruction programs, recognize the sovereignty of Kuwait, account for missing Kuwaitis, return Kuwaiti property and end support for international terrorism.

8. http://www.un.org/sg/biography.shtml.

admitting of new members and matters concerning the U.N. budget. A simple majority is sufficient for all other matters. In recent years, the U.N. has been trying to reach decisions through consensus, rather than by taking a formal vote.[9]

D. The Economic and Social Council, http://www.un.org/ecosoc/

The Economic and Social Council is under jurisdiction of the General Assembly and coordinates the economic and social work of the United Nations system. The Council consists of 54 members, elected by the General Assembly for three-year terms.[10] Under the U.N. Charter, the Council has authority to select its own rules of procedure and elect its president.[11] ECOSOC is responsible for over 70% of the human and financial resources of the entire U.N. system. The U.N. swims in an ocean of acronyms. You will get used to them as you work with them.

In relation to the structure of the United Nations, the Economic and Social Council serves as a forum for discussing international economic and social issues and for formulating policy recommendations. The Economic and Social Council can invite any member of the United Nations to participate, with-

9. Rules of Procedure of the General Assembly (U.N. Doc. A/520/Rev.15 + Amend.1 + Amend.2; Sales number 85.-I.13).

10. U.N. Charter, ch. X, art. 61.

11. U.N. Charter, ch. X, art. 72.

out vote, in its deliberations on any matter of particular concern to that state.[12]

ECOSOC oversees the work of the 14 U.N. Specialized agencies, functionaly commissions and regional commissions. The five regional commissions are responsible for promoting economic development and cooperation in their respective regions. Other commissions reporting to ECOSOC focus on issues including social development, the status of women, crime prevention, narcotic drugs and environmental protection. It has the power to make or initiate studies and reports on these issues. It also has the power to assist in the preparations and organization of major international conferences in the economic and social and related fields and to facilitate a coordinated follow-up to these conferences.

E.   The Trusteeship Council, http://www.un. org/documents/tc.htm

The Trusteeship Council was established under the U.N. Charter to oversee the preparation of the Trust Territories for either self-government or independence. By 1994, the Territories achieved this status, either as separate States or by joining neighboring independent countries. The Trusteeship Council's work culminated in 1994 with the independence of Palau. The Council currently consists of the five permanent members of the Security Council and need only schedule further meetings by

12. U.N. Charter, ch. X, art. 69.

its own decision or at the request of a majority of its members or the General Assembly or the Security Council.

F. Specialized Agencies and Other Programs, http://www.un.org/aboutun/chart.html

There are several organizations functioning as specialized agencies worldwide that work in concert with the U.N. For instance, the International Monetary Fund, the World Bank, World Health Organization and eleven other independent organizations collaborate with U.N. through cooperative agreements. These organizations were developed by intergovernmental agreement and function autonomously. Together they cover a comprehensive range of international issues including culture, economics, health, and education.

There are additional easily recognizable U.N. offices, programs and funds including the U.N. Children's Fund (UNICEF), Office of the U.N. High Commissioner for Refugees (UNHCR), and the U.N. Development Program (UNDP). Each of these entities report to either the General Assembly or to the Economic and Social Council. While each has its own governing bodies, budgets and secretariats, they all work in collaboration with the U.N. as a whole. Depending on the role of the U.N. agency, the policies issued may be binding on members as formal international law or may serve as policy recommendations for the construction of binding international law.

G. The International Court of Justice, http://www.icj-cij.org/

The International Court of Justice, sometimes referred to as the World Court, serves as a tribunal to the U.N. In addition to providing advisory opinions[13] to the General Assembly and the Security Council, the Court primarily serves as a venue for legal disputes submitted by States. The General Assembly and the Security Council jointly elect fifteen judges to sit on the bench for a term of nine years. The Court may not include more than one judge from any one nationality. There is no mandate under the U.N. Charter requiring States to appear before the Court. However, once they accede or give consent to do so, countries must abide by the Court's decisions.[14] Recognizing that the Court's jurisdiction is voluntary is crucial to comprehending the role of the Court. Even States that are not members of the U.N., may be brought in as parties if approved by the General Assembly and Security Council.[15] If the Court does not include a judge possessing the nationality of a State party to a case, that State may appoint a person to sit as a judge ad hoc for the purpose of the case.

8.5 The U.N.'s Impact on Human Rights Law

In addition to adopting the U.N. Charter in 1948, the General Assembly also enacted the Universal

13. U.N. Charter, ch. XIV, art. 96, para. 1.

14. U.N. Charter, ch. XIV, art. 94.

15. U.N. Charter, ch. XIV, art. 93, para. 2.

Declaration of Human Rights (UDHR). The Declaration is used today as a charter of the Human Rights Movement. The UDHR recognizes every individual's right to life, liberty, and personal security without distinction by "race, color, sex, language, religion, political or other opinion, national or social origin, property, birth or other status."[16] The Declaration has been a powerful tool for the General Assembly in implementing standards for protecting the rights of women, children, disabled persons, minorities, migrant workers and other vulnerable groups, against discriminatory practices. Although the UDHR doesn't have the formal binding authority to influence State behavior that the U.N. Charter does, it has gained acceptance as the standard bearer of international human rights norms—or the customary international law of human rights.

8.6 The U.N.'s Impact on International Law

The efforts of the U.N. to promote social and economic development have evolved into an international body of law through conventions, treaties and standards. The treaties have been used widely to create laws governing international relations. Furthermore, the United Nations has sponsored over 500 multilateral agreements that are legally binding when ratified by individual countries. Among the issues addressed by these agreements are: protection of the environment, regulation of migrant la-

16. Universal Declaration of Human Rights, art. 2 and art. 3.

bor, the curbing of drug trafficking, and combating terrorism.

The U.N. has experienced a significant degree of difficulty in establishing an authoritative role in preventing conflicts. An optimist can point with pride to those instances where U.N. intervention has helped, a pessimist can look to the continuing conflicts and horrors that can be found in the world. At this point the U.N. is the only hope. But its success lies within the control of the Member States, especially those permanent members of the Security Council which wield great practical power. Conflicts aside, it is important to note that in collaboration with other agencies, the U.N. has seen substantial success as a catalyst for social and economic development around the world. The U.N. has also promoted normative standards, such as encouraging lawful interactions among all countries. The elements are in place, it is up to the nations of the world to use them.

8.7   U.N. Documents and Publications

Researching U.N. documents used to require a trip to a library that provided access to an enormous paper collection of documents or a microfiche collection. Today's researcher can obtain many U.N. documents on the web at no cost. While there is access to U.N. documents on the web, keep in mind that you may still need to use a print or microfiche collection for some older or more obscure documents. These collections will be reviewed at the end of this section.

U.N. documents are defined as follows: "A document is a text submitted to a principal organ or a subsidiary organ of the United Nations for consideration by it, usually in connection with item(s) on its agenda."[17]

The U.N. documentation system is a massive enterprise and the legal researcher will never touch many of the documents issued by the U.N. An excellent overview of the legal materials issued by the United Nations is contained in the *United Nations Documentation: Research Guide, International Law*.[18] This guide "defines the principal U.N. bodies working in the area of international law; identifies the document series symbols attached to their working documents, as well as the major types of documents and publications they produce; and gives some basic tips for conducting topical searches in the Library's online database UNBISnet."[19] The principal legal bodies of the U.N. are the Sixth Committee of the General Assembly, the International Law Commission, and the United Nations Commission on International Trade Law (UNCITRAL). See the United Nations Documentation: Research Guide[20] for an overview of the documents

17. http://www.un.org/ Depts/dhl/resguide/symbol. htm#define.

18. http://www.un.org/ Depts/dhl/resguide/specil.htm.

19. See Maureen Ratynski Andersen, *Where to Begin . . . When You Don't Know How to Start: Tips for Researching U.N. Legal Materials*, 31 Int'l J. Legal Info. 264 (2003).

20. http://www.un.org/ Depts/dhl/resguide/specil. htm#legal.

and publications issued by the principal legal bodies of the U.N.

A.   Getting Started

To better understand how U.N. documents are numbered and organized, it is good to have at least a basic understanding of the structure of the organization. Hopefully, you have read the introduction to the U.N. at the beginning of this chapter. To supplement this outline, you should also consult the *United Nations Documentation: Research Guide.*[21] One of the first things this guide does is explain document symbols and how they are structured. Each U.N. document has its own unique symbol, like an address, and this address is needed for both locating the document in a collection (in any format) and is also useful for citation purposes. As stated in the research guide:

"A symbol is a combination of numbers and letters which serves as a unique identifier for a United Nations document. It generally does not give any significant indication of the subject of a document."[22]

It is important to note that the symbol remains the same no matter the language of the document. So, if you find a document in Spanish and need it in English, the symbol on the Spanish version can be used to locate the English document.

21.   http://www.un.org/ Depts/dhl/resguide/.

22.   http://www.un.org/ Depts/dhl/resguide/symbol. htm.

The first component of the symbol is the abbreviation for the parent organ or body. The second element indicates the subsidiary body. Special components indicate the nature of the document and the final component indicates if there have been modifications.

For example, A/CONF.157/PC/63/Add.4

A/:	General Assembly
CONF.157/:	World Conference on Human Rights
PC/:	Preparatory Committee
63/:	Document number 63
Add.4:	Addendum 4

The research guide mentioned above provides greater detail on U.N. document symbols and should be consulted when trying to decipher an unfamiliar document symbol.

There are other document numbers to be aware of when using U.N. documents. Some documents have "sales numbers." These are usually publications that are of general interest.

Some publications might have both a sales number and a U.N. symbol. For the most part, the researcher does not need to worry about sales numbers. An example of a sales number is 06. v. 2= 2007 edition of Multilateral Treaties Deposited with the Secretary–General.

For more assistance with researching U.N. documents, see *Selected U.N. Resources & Research Tools: Overview and Search Tips for Legal Research,* by Wiltrud Harms at UC Berkeley Law

Library.[23] This easy to use guide allows you to quickly figure out which resource to use for your U.N. legal research problem.

B. Locating Documents

1. Official Records

These are documents submitted to or issued by the major U.N. bodies during a given session or year. *The Bluebook* says you should always cite to official records, but that can be a problem since they are not published until after the session concludes. Official records include meeting records; resolutions; reports of major organs, committees and commissions as well as the budget and financial reports. It is easy to identify these documents since they are identified as such on the title page.

When you have a document and a document symbol, you may be tempted to conduct a Google search to locate this document on the web. While this may work some of the time, it may lead to chaos. A better approach is to use the collections of documents provided by the U.N.

2. Full-text Documents

ODS (Official Document System)[24]

"ODS covers all types of official United Nations documentation, beginning in 1993. Older U.N. docu-

23. http://www.law. berkeley.edu/library/online/ guides/international_foreign/ UNResourcesResearchTools. pdf.

24. http://documents.un. org/welcome.asp?language=E.

ments are, however, added to the system on a daily basis. ODS also provides access to the resolutions of the General Assembly, Security Council, Economic and Social Council and the Trusteeship Council from 1946 onwards. The system does not contain press releases, U.N. sales publications, the United Nations Treaty Series or information brochures issued by the Department of Public Information."[25]

If you have the document symbol and it falls within the date range mentioned above, the easiest thing to do is to use the "simple" search screen and type in the document number in the box where it says "Symbol"—(see Figure 1).

25. http://documents.un. org/welcome.asp?language=E.

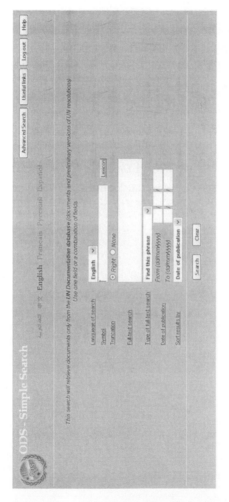

Figure 1: ODS Simple Search

For example, suppose that you need the United Nations Declaration on Human Cloning, U.N. Doc. A/RES/59/280 (2004). Using ODS, you can simply type "A/RES/59/280" into the box indicated above and click on "search."

By clicking on "A/RES/59/280" (see Figure 2) you will see the screen below and you can display and download the document in any of the available languages as well as obtain other information about the document such as, complete title, publication date, and subjects (see Figure 3).

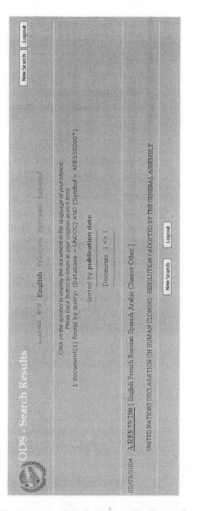

Figure 2: ODS Search Result

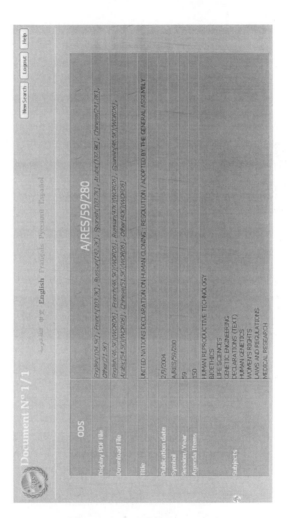

Figure 3: ODS Record

The main U.N. website[26] can also be used for obtaining some documents. Select the "Documentation, Maps" button at the top of the page and you will be linked to the "U.N. Documentation Centre."[27] From this page, you can access some of the most frequently used documents: General Assembly, Security Council and Economic and Social Council resolutions, press releases, Secretary General reports, and other selected documents.

The U.N. Documentation Centre website will also link you to ODS (mentioned above) and other collections of documents.

While ODS and the U.N. Documentation Centre offer many documents, you may still need to use other tools for locating the U.N. document symbol or do some searching for documents by subject or issuing body.

3.   Document Indexes

UNBISnet[28] is an electronic catalog of U.N. documents and publications indexed by the Dag Hammarskjöld Library and the Library of the U.N. Office at Geneva. It also includes commercial publications and other non-U.N. sources held in the collection of the Dag Hammarskjöld Library. The coverage is from 1979 onward, but older documents are added on a regular basis. UNBISnet also provides access to some full text documents, including resolutions adopted by the General Assembly, the Economic and Social Council and the Security Council from 1946 onward.

26. http://www.un.org/english/.

27. http://www.un.org/documents/.

28. http://unbisnet.un.org.

Access U.N.[29] is an electronic index to U.N. documents including Official Records, draft resolutions, meeting records, sales publications, and the U.N. Treaty Series citations. It also includes the full-text of several thousand U.N. documents. It covers 1944 to present.

C. U.N. Resolutions

Sometimes the researcher needs primary documents like the resolutions from the major U.N. organs (General Assembly, Security Council, and Economic and Social Council). "United Nations resolutions are formal expressions of the opinion or will of United Nations organs. They generally consist of two clearly defined sections: a preamble and an operative part. The preamble generally presents the considerations on the basis of which action is taken, an opinion expressed or a directive given. The operative part states the opinion of the organ or the action to be taken."[30]

Fortunately, most of these resolutions are available from the U.N. Documentation Centre.[31] From here, there is access to the following:

General Assembly, A/RES, 1946 to present.

Security Council, S/RES, 1946 to present.

Economic and Social Council, 1992–2004.

29. A subscription database which is available from many academic law libraries, http://infoweb.newsbank.com.

30. http://www.un.org/Depts/dhl/resguide/scres.htm.

31. http://www.un.org/documents/index.html.

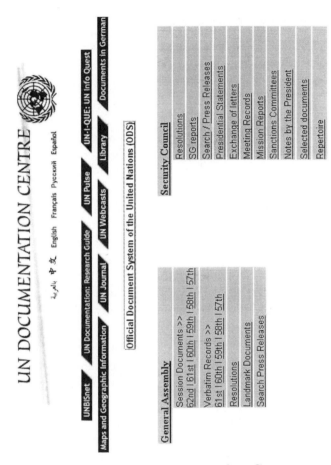

Figure 4: UN Documentation Centre

For access to resolutions not available from the U.N. Documentation Centre, try ODS or UNBISnet. Resolutions are also available in the official records at the end of each session and in other print sources.

D. Treaties

Treaties are another important source of law sought for by the legal researcher. The U.N. Charter mandates that every treaty and international agreement entered into by Member States must be registered with the U.N. Secretary General. While Member States invariably do not follow this directive, most treaties are deposited. The official source for these treaties is the *United Nations Treaty Series* (U.N.T.S.), available in print and through the database called United Nations Treaty Collection.[32] The print version of U.N.T.S. covers 1946–date, with a lag time of a few years. The electronic version contains over 158,000 treaties, covering 1946–2005[33], but the researcher may need to use the print version to fill in any gaps.

The predecessor series is called the *League of Nations Treaty Series* (L.N.T.S.) and it covers 1920–1946; this set is available in print and through the United Nations Treaty Collection online.

The United Nations Treaty Collection is the electronic collection of treaties and agreements. The database contains several very important resources, including *Status of Multilateral Treaties Deposited with the Secretary General*, U.N.T.S. and L.N.T.S., texts of recently deposited multilateral treaties, and U.N.T.S. cumulative indexes. *Status of Multilateral*

---

32. http://untreaty.un.org/.   **33.** http://untreaty.un.org/english/overview.asp.

Treaties Deposited with the Secretary General contains the current status of over 500 multilateral treaties deposited with the Secretary–General. This information includes conclusion and entry into force dates; the participants (parties); the signature and ratification dates; the text of reservations and declarations; and a link to the text of the treaty. This publication is also available in print, but the electronic version will always be more up to date.

Many U.N. treaties and agreements are available in other collections (both print and electronic); however, if possible, use the version from the U.N.T.S.

Some U.N. bodies provide access to specialized collections of treaties. For example, the U.N. High Commissioner for Human Rights provides access to U.N. human rights treaties.[34] The U.N. Environment Programme (UNEP) also provides a collection of international environmental treaties.

For more information on researching treaties, see Chapter 4 of this Nutshell.

8.8   Other Collections

As noted in the beginning of this section, there may be an occasion when you cannot locate the document on the web. In those instances, you may need to go to a library that has a print or microfiche collection[35]. Some libraries are designated as United

34. http://www2.ohchr.org/english/law/index.htm.

35. The microfiche is published by Readex and is available in many academic libraries.

Nations "depositories" and have more extensive collections than non-depositories. A reference librarian who works at such a depository library can be an enormously helpful guide.

8.9 Beyond the Documents: Books and Articles

There will come a time when you will need some commentary or analysis on topics handled by the U.N. or some explanation about the U.N. system or a particular body. Some of the better books on U.N. law and practice are listed below. These materials are not available electronically, but they should be available in many academic law libraries.

Charter of the United Nations: A Commentary (Bruno Simma ed., 2nd ed. 2002) is the best source for commentary and analysis of the U.N. Charter.

Benedetto Conforti, *The Law and Practice of the United Nations* (3rd rev. ed. 2005) provides legal analysis of membership, structure, origins, and practice.

Max Planck Yearbook of United Nations Law (1998–) focuses on the activities of the U.N. in the field of international law. Available on HeinOnline.

The United Nations: Law and Practice (Franz Cede & Lilly Sucharipa–Behrmann eds., 2001) provides useful information on the historical and legal framework for activities of the U.N. in a single volume.

Yearbook of the United Nations (1946/47–) provides a detailed history for each year. It includes resolutions and gives useful references to important reports and documents. Many U.N. bodies and institutions issue their own yearbooks, such as *Yearbook of the International Law Commission*.

When doing research on a topic, you may want to search library catalogs or look for articles on the topic. UNBISnet (described above) does provide information about books and articles on U.N. bodies and topics. Journal articles are a good source of information on topics covered by the U.N. For more assistance on locating relevant journal literature, see Chapter 10 of this Nutshell.

CHAPTER 9

OTHER INTERNATIONAL ORGANIZATIONS

9.1   Introduction

In recent decades, international organizations, meaning both intergovernmental organizations (IGOs) and nongovernmental organizations (NGOs), have developed into important players in the international legal community. Your research problem may center on one of these organizations or you may need a document produced by one of them. Therefore locating information that concerns them and finding their documentation is a necessary skill for one working in the area of international legal research. This Nutshell has already discussed the United Nations and the European

Union, two international bodies which exert an enormous amount of influence in the world and which issue an impressive amount of documents and information. The focus of this chapter is to set out the basics of researching IGOs and NGOs generally and to describe some strategies for locating relevant documentation. We will provide general background and take one very large IGO, the World Trade Organization, and one very prominent NGO, Amnesty International, as exemplars.

According to the Union of International Associations, there are over 61,000 international organizations–IGOs, NGOs, and other bodies.[1] Generally, an IGO is an "association of States established by and based upon a treaty, which pursues common aims and which has its own special organs to fulfill particular functions within the organization."[2] There are many examples of IGOs. The United Nations is the most well-known, and the Universal Postal Union is the oldest.[3]

Most of these organizations have the following characteristics:

> An IGO has *international legal status* (privileges, immunities, rights and duties) which are based upon its founding charter, constitution or statute.

1. See http://www.diversit as.org/db/x.php.

2. Rudolf L. Bindschedler, "International Organizations General Aspects," *in* 2 *Encyclopedia of Public International Law* 1289 (1992).

3. Treaty Concerning the Formation of a General Postal Union, Oct. 9, 1987, 19 Stat. 577, 1 Bevans 29; revised by the Convention for the Formation of a Universal Postal Union, June 1, 1878, 20 Stat. 734, 1 Bevans 51.

As such, an IGO can enter into international agreements with other IGOs or with States.

An IGO usually has a *legislative body* which creates legal acts (decisions, resolutions, directives, etc.) which may bind the IGO and its Member States under international law. Most of these legislative acts do not supersede national law (with the exception of the EU).

An IGO may have a *dispute resolution mechanism* or body which is empowered to resolve disputes among its Member States.

The IGO usually has an *executive body* or secretariat which facilitates the operations of the IGO.

The World Trade Organization, for example, was created by the Marrakesh Treaty, signed on April 15, 1994.[4] It has a Secretariat headed by the Director–General; the General Council is the WTO's highest-level decision-making body and meets regularly to carry out the work of the organization, whereas the topmost decision-making body is the Ministerial Conference and it meets less often, at least once every two years; and the Dispute Settlement Body settles trade disputes between the Member States.[5] The members are sovereign nations, each entering into the organization by choice.

4. Final Act Embodying the Results of the Uruguay Round of Multilateral Trade Negotiations, Apr. 15, 1994, 1867 U.N.T.S. 14, 33 I.L.M. 1143 (1994).

5. WTO Organization Chart, http://www.wto.org/english/thewto_e/whatis_e/tif_e/org2_e.htm.

Many of an organization's characteristics are mandated by the organization's founding instrument. These instruments can be called a treaty, convention, charter, or constitution. Since IGOs are made up of nation-state members and concern high-profile topics they often have well-developed information systems. The WTO is an extreme example, but you will find organizational information for most IGOs.

On the other hand, organizations established by individuals or associations of individuals are called nongovernmental organizations (NGOs). NGOs are not endowed with governmental powers and cannot enter into treaties or international agreements.[6] NGOs vary in size and influence. Some of the larger groups can exercise considerable pressure in international policy debates. Often an NGO takes an advocacy position and lobbies for its principles. NGOs such as Amnesty International and Greenpeace are good examples. Not all NGOs are so high profile, some concern quite banal topics.

For more information on the intricacies of international organizations, see Philippe Sands and Pierre Klein, *Bowett's Law of International Institutions* (5th ed. 2001) or *International Organizations* (Jan Klabbers ed., 2005).

9.2   Bibliographies and Research Guides

Before entering into a research problem that concerns an IGO or an NGO, it is vital that you

6. *Parry and Grant Encyclopaedic Dictionary of International Law* 347(2003).

understand the nature of the organization and the context in which it operates. Seek out a research guide or an article about the international organization that will help you understand the structure of the organization and the documentation it issues. Follow the oldest research advice in the world and know the territory before you enter into it. There is plenty of help available. Many of the most useful guides are available on the web:

- ASIL Guide to Electronic Resources for International Law: International Organizations.[7] This chapter has some handy tips on locating documents and information. It is assembled by researchers who are dedicated to giving you the most helpful guidance possible. No axes to grind here, just great information.

- Non–Governmental Organizations Research Guide (Duke University).[8] Yet another example of a law school library stepping up to help the researcher.

- International Organizations/Nongovernmental Organizations Research/Subject Guide (Emory University).[9] Someone has done a lot of work for you here.

7. http://www.asil.org/resource/intorg1.htm.

8. http://docs.lib.duke.edu/igo/guides/ngo/.

9. http://web.library.emory.edu/subjects/socsci/polsci/igongo.html.

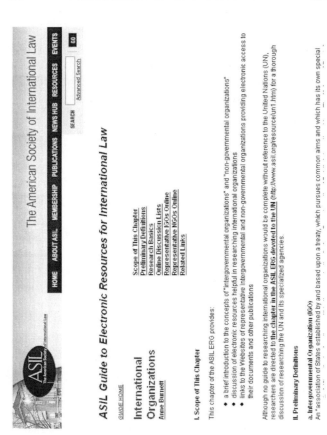

Figure 1: ASIL Guide

Many folks have posted organization specific guides on the web to assist you with researching various organizations, such as History, Role and Activities of the Council of Europe: Facts, Figures and Information Sources.[10] Topical guides may also

10.   http://www.nyu
lawglobal.org/globalex/
Council_of_Europe.htm.

provide information about researching the documentation from various IGOs and NGOs. For example, the human rights chapter of the ASIL Guide to Electronic Resources for International Law provides in-depth information on various human rights organizations.[11]

9.3 Background Information

When researching an international organization, there may be a need for what might be styled nitty gritty information: historical background, function, structure, addresses, names of key officials, names of member countries, and a short list of publications of international organizations. If the organization has its own website, you may find what you need; but some organizations are too small, some websites are too lacking in content, and besides, you should know the general guides that have earned the respect of researchers. The *Encyclopedia of Associations: International Organizations* (1989–) provides addresses, phone numbers, etc. plus budget, membership, and publication information. See also, *The Europa Directory of International Organizations* (1999–) or the *Yearbook of International Organizations* (1967–) which provides contact information as well as information about meetings, membership, and publications. These are familiar tools that possess the authority granted by researchers who use them.

11.   http://www.asil.org/
resource/humrts1.htm.

Most international organizations have some sort of web presence. A quick way of locating the appropriate website is by doing a Google search by the name or acronym of the organizations or by using one of the web directories mentioned above. Larger organizations use their websites as the primary mechanism for providing information about the organization and for distributing documentation.

Use directories or compilations of sites to locate the correct website for an IGO or NGO. Once again, academic libraries have compiled this information for you and made it available for free:

- International Governmental Organizations (Northwestern University)[12]

- International Agencies and Information on the Web (University of Michigan)[13]

9.4   Documents and Publications

Many IGOs issue publications and documents that may be of interest to the legal researcher: founding documents (treaties, charters, statutes); treaties where the IGO is a party, treaties where the IGO is the sponsor; legal acts, proceedings, documents issued by the IGO's legislative body; and decisions of the IGO's adjudicative body.

Again, the WTO provides a good example by looking at its publications and documents. By look-

12. http://www.library. nwu.edu/govpub/resource/ internat/igo.html.

13. http://www.lib.umich. edu/govdocs/intl.html.

ing at its website, you locate information on the structure and functions of the organization. The "Documents Gateway" provides access to its legal instruments and official documents. The GATT, the predecessor of the WTO, the quasi-international organization that existed until 1995, issued documents through a microfiche collection.[14] The process for locating documents was quite cumbersome and many documents were never made available because they were considered "restricted." The WTO makes many more documents available and the best mechanism for accessing them is through the "Documents Online" facility on the web.[15] Pre-configured searches can be done, usually based on the issuing body or by topic.

14. Some GATT documents are available on the WTO website and through the GATT Digital Archive, http://gatt.stanford.edu/page/home.

15. http://www.wto.org/english/docs_e/docs_e.htm.

Search Documents Online

Anti-dumping documents use the code G/ADP/* (where * takes additional values)
These links open a new window: allow a moment for the results to appear.

> **help** with downloading these documents

- **Annual reports** of the Committee on Anti-dumping Practices to the General Council (Document code varies)   > search
- **Minutes** of the meetings of the Committee on Anti-dumping Practices (Document code G/ADP/M/*)   > search
- **Working documents** of the Committee on Anti-dumping Practices (Document code G/ADP/W/*)

  | Select a year... ▾ | > search

- **Reports** of the Committee on Anti-dumping Practices under Article 16.4 of the agreement (searches for document code G/ADP/N/* and keywords "reports under Article 16.4")

  | Select a year... ▾ | > search

- **Semi-annual reports** of the Committee on Anti-dumping Practices under Article 16.4 of the agreement (searches for document code G/ADP/N/* and keywords "Semi-annual report")

  | Select a year... ▾ | > search

- **Disputes** (requests for consultations) involving anti-dumping (Document code G/ADP/D*)   > search
- **Notifications** by individual members on anti-dumping (Document code G/ADP/N/*)

  | Select a country then click on search... ▾ | > search

You can perform more sophisticated searches from the Documents Online search facility (opens in new window) by defining multiple search criteria such as document code, full text search or document date.

Figure 2: WTO Preconfigured Search Options

Otherwise, the researcher can browse or search the entire collection. An example of a "catalogue record" for a document indicates the kind of information provided for each document in the database:

Collection	G	*Access Level*	**Public**
Symbol	**G/SPS/GEN/598**	*Status*	
Date	**14/10/2005**	*Derestricted on*	
Doc#	**05–4697**	*File*	**g/sps/gen598.doc**
English Title	Committee on Sanitary and Phytosanitary Measures—Notifications Issued during the Month of September 2005—Note by the Secretariat		
French Title			
Spanish Title			
Contents	Notifications Issued during the Month of September 2005—Note by the Secretariat		
Subjects	SANITARY AND PHYTOSANITARY REGULATIONS		
Countries	Australia ; Brazil ; Canada ; Chile ; China ; Chinese Taipei ; Colombia ; Egypt ; European Union ; Indonesia ; Jamaica ; Kenya ; Korea (Republic) ; Mexico ; Nepal ; New Zealand ; Sri Lanka ; Switzerland ; Thailand ; Trinidad and Tobago ; United States		
WTO Bodies	Committee on Sanitary and Phytosanitary Measures		
Articles	SPS 07 Annex B		
Organizations			
Products			
Meeting date			
References			
Pages English	9		
Pages French	0		
Pages Spanish	0		
Document Types	Note—Secretariat		

Like the UN and EU, the WTO has an extensive document collection utilizing a unique document organization based on the use of symbols. We will examine these as an example of what you might find when working with an IGO. There is no need to tremble when you encounter alpha-numerics such as these, see how they make sense below:

Examples of different WTO document symbols:

G/L/71
GPA/SPEC/2/Rev.1
IP/C/W/15
OFFICE(00)/39
S/ENQ/9
WT/CTE/W/31

Each symbol is made up of a combination of letters, numbers and suffixes. Letters are used to identify collections, series, types and the status of documents while numbers are used to indicate sequential order. Three letter ISO standard codes are also used to identify Members (e.g. POL for Poland, ZWE for Zimbabwe, etc.). All documents are numbered in chronological order of issue and some documents may have more than one symbol.

For example, IP/C/W/34/Add.3/Suppl.3—What does it all mean? That string of letters and numbers translates as the third supplement to the third addendum to the thirty-fourth working document issued by the Council for Trade Related Aspects of Intellectual Property Rights (part of the Intellectual Property document collection):

IP = Collection
C = Series
W = Type
34; **3**; **3** = Sequential numbers
Add.; **Suppl.** = Status

The more sophisticated IGOs have intricate documentation systems like this one. The United Nations and the European Union have systems that can be even more obscure in appearance. There are some books and research guides which explain the nature and organization of these documentary systems. See *Guide to International Legal Research* (2002–) and *Information Systems of International Governmental Organizations* (2nd ed. 1997).

Another approach to understanding these symbols would be to use a research guide or article that focuses on the organization in question. Such a guide may explain a documentation system or list depositories or libraries where research assistance is available. For example, WTO and GATT Research[16] provides detailed guidance on both official and unofficial sources for GATT/WTO documents. But this is an area where a trained librarian may be your best bet. Do not spin your wheels, ask for help.

Be prepared to use unofficial sources which reproduce or compile important legal documents. Sometimes commentators or private publishers just do a better job at making information available. Of course, when using such sources it may be possible to access only parts of documents. Many of the documents issued by IGOs are in subject compilations.

Periodicals are good source for information about documents and publications. Periodicals and reports that are actually issued by the organization are an informative source. Articles that appear in law reviews and texts can also provide great background

16. http://www.law.nyu. edu/library/wtoguide.html

information; check out Chapter 10 for help on that score.

NGOs tend to publish many reports, newsletters, and documents that may not have a great deal of legal weight, but are valuable to the researcher because they may document economic and social conditions and provide analysis which indicate the sources or issues. Such reports may focus on a particular country or on a topic. These materials may describe the work of the NGO or report on a particular issue or situation. Effective methods for locating such documents are the library catalogs and secondary sources discussed elsewhere in this Nutshell. Many law reviews and books will cite to documents published by NGOs, especially in the area of human rights and environmental protection.

An example of an NGO with an extensive document system is Amnesty International (AI). Many libraries collect the documents and reports issued by AI and so they are publicly available in these libraries. AI has also made many of them available for free on its website.[17] Many of the documents contain a number referred to as AI Index, for example "AI Index: ASA 13/010/2005." This refers to the region (Asia-Pacific) and the number of the report (the last portion indicating the year). Other index

17. The Amnesty International library contains an archive of most reports, news releases and urgent actions published from 1996 to date, http://web.amnesty.org/library/engindex.

numbers may have a topical designation rather than a regional one.

9.5   LexisNexis and Westlaw

Neither of these services provides access to much in the way of IGO and NGO documentation. However, for selected IGOs, some materials are available, such as GATT and WTO panel reports.

9.6   Some Final Thoughts

Finding documents produced by IGOs and NGOs can be difficult and frustrating. There is a general lack of good indexing, abstracting, and bibliographies for these documents. Many IGOs have their own organization and classification schemes. Even if you have what you think is a valid citation, the document may not actually be available in a library's collection (they cannot be purchased through regular channels). Often the documents that are made available are not the ones legal researchers are most interested in. Also, often the publication of official documents can be quite slow.

But the Internet is making things much better and there are many libraries and advocacy groups trying to assist you. Take heart, you will find what you need.

CHAPTER 10

COMMENTARY AND ANALYSIS

10.1 Introduction

If researching international law is new to you, consider starting your research with sources that contain commentary and analysis—books, articles, working papers, and other secondary sources. Reviewing commentary and analysis early in the research process will provide you with an introduction to an unfamiliar topic, provide citations to relevant laws and documents, allow you to gain an understanding of the terms of art and other vocabulary, and keep you abreast of new legal developments. Gaining command of the context of your research is important, no matter what field you work in, but in questions of international law, where intuition may lead you down the wrong path, it is of special importance.

Each day, access to e-books, electronic journals, and other sources through the internet progresses forward. As this Chapter is going through its final edit, Amazon is announcing its new "Kindle" project,[1] and more is surely to come. However, much of the best commentary and analysis, i.e. the very contextual material that you need for international research, is still primarily in print. Projects like Google Books,[2] Project Guttenberg,[3] the Internet Archives' Million Book Project,[4] and Open Content Alliance[5] hold great promise, but these projects contain few relevant sources for international law research (not to mention for foreign or comparative law). There is more available if your library subscribes to some of the specific e-book collections, such as The Making of Modern Law[6] or Early English Books Online.[7] These two are especially rich sets, but as such they carry sizeable price tags, so only the best collections currently possess them. Some general e-book collections, like Ebrary[8] or MyILibrary,[9] contain some books on various inter-

---

1. http://www.amazon.com/Kindle–Amazons–Wireless–Reading–Device/dp/B000FI73MA.

2. http://books.google.com.

3. http://www.gutenberg.org/wiki/Main_Page.

4. http://www.archive.org/details/millionbooks.

5. http://www.opencontentalliance.org/

6. http://www.gale.com/ModernLaw/.

7. http://eebo.chadwyck.com/home.

8. http://www.ebrary.com/corp/libraries.jsp.

9. http://www.myilibrary.com/.

national law topics. Though it smacks of a romantic attachment to the ways things used to be done, there is still no substitute for a good print collection–at least not yet.

10.2 Library Catalogs

Indeed to begin research on a topic that is unfamiliar we recommend that most venerable of tools, the library catalog. Trust us, there are still instances where a catalog, assembled by subject specialists, will serve you better than a Google search. Be smart and search the catalogs of your own library as well as catalogs of libraries from around the country and even around the world. The major bibliographic database in the United States is OCLC (the Online Computer Library Center).[10] OCLC includes the records of academic libraries, law firm libraries, and other libraries in the US and a few from other countries. WorldCat is OCLC's catalog of books and other materials, and it's available in many academic and public libraries in the United States. One search on your computer opens the doors to collections all over the world.

Most library catalogs allow you to search by author, title, keyword and subject. If you know of one book on your topic, you can find others by searching the subjects associated with that one source. Most catalogs also allow you to limit your search by language, date, and material type (book, journal, electronic resource, etc.). Some catalogs provide

10. http://www.oclc.org/ home.

even more advanced features, such as tables of contents, links to electronic versions of the materials, and the ability to download and save records. The librarians who assemble these online catalogs are working hard to provide you with every possible aid.

Books are not the only place to begin. Journal articles are an important part of international legal research. They can provide good introductions to topics or detailed analysis. Even if you find the text of a journal article to be of little help, the article may contain citations to a plethora of other sources. The footnotes of a journal article are sometimes more valuable than the text. Someone has done a great deal of work gathering sources for you. Of course, a journal article may also provide guidance as to the principles of customary international law.

Here is an important tip for locating a broad range of legal journal literature in international law. Do not rely solely on the full-text law review collections that you find on the LexisNexis and Westlaw databases. If you want to do thorough research, then you must use journal indexes to locate relevant literature. Indexes are not very popular these days. They usually require you to master a different set of search protocols and they may give you only a citation to what you need, with no link to the text. This results in the dreaded two-step research process. You find the citation and then you have to go find the text. But there is value in these indexes. They provide access to a broader range of journal literature and therefore include many journals that are not available full-text on LexisNexis or Westlaw. Consequently, by searching indexes, you might locate more articles on point. When doing research in international law it maybe the more obscure journal that contains exactly what you need.

Increasingly journal indexes are available electronically, although each journal index operates in a slightly different manner. How to truncate words or the use of connectors (and, or, within, etc.) can vary from index to index. Be sure to consult the "help" screens for information on how to search properly. (We know that no one ever actually consults the "help" screens, but we feel obliged to try to get you to do so). A few minutes spent reading this information can save you from doing fruitless searches.

In order to locate the text of the articles you find by searching the indexes, you may need to search one of the aforementioned online catalogs by the title of the journal to determine if your library owns the print and/or provides access to the electronic. It is important to note that not all journals are available electronically and the article you want may not be available from a database. Therefore, you may need to go to a library and retrieve the print version of the journal.

10.3 Legal Journal Indexes

Most of the databases listed below are only available by subscription. Luckily, most law school libraries do provide access to at least one of them. Some are also available on LexisNexis and Westlaw.

Index to Legal Periodicals and Books (commonly referred to as ILP). ILP contains citations from more than 1,000 legal periodicals dating from 1982 published in the United States, Canada, Ireland, Great Britain, Australia and New Zealand. The print edition covers 1908 to present. ILP is available on LexisNexis and on Westlaw, and the web.[11] Access to a retrospective collection is also available through the Wilson web version of the database and it covers 1908–1981.[12] It is the old warhorse of legal indexes and is found in most libraries.

Legal Resource Index (commonly referred to as LRI). LRI indexes approximately 875 legal publications from the United States, Canada, Great Britain, New Zealand and Australia. It also covers law-related articles from more than 1,000 additional business and general interest periodicals. Coverage begins in 1980. It is also available in print as *Current Law Index*. LRI is available on LexisNexis, Westlaw and through the web as Legaltrac.[13]

While there is some overlap in the coverage available from ILP and LRI, it is worthwhile to search both indexes. It takes a few moments to master the search techniques required by each but it is fairly intuitive.

11. http://www.hwwilson. com/Databases/legal.htm.

12. http://www.hwwilson. com/Databases/legal_retro. htm.

13. http://www.gale.com/ tlist/sb5088.html.

Index to Foreign Legal Periodicals (commonly referred to as IFLP). IFLP is a multilingual index to articles and book reviews appearing in approximately 460 legal journals published worldwide. The print edition covers the time period from 1960 on and the electronic version covers 1985 to the present. IFLP is available on the web via Ovid[14] and on Westlaw, but the Westlaw version is not accessible with an academic password. Since it indexes journals from all over the world, do not be surprised if you pull up an article that is not in English.

Legal Journals Index (commonly referred to as LJI). LJI indexes over 400 journals from the UK and Europe. Coverage dates from 1986 on. The print versions of this index (*Legal Journals Index* and *European Legal Journals Index)* discontinued in 1999. *Legal Journals Index* is available on Westlaw and via the web.

Current Index to Legal Periodicals (commonly referred to as CILP). CILP provides access to over 570 university legal publications and other law journals. CILP is assembled by the staff of the Marian Gallagher Library at the University of Washington and is quite reliable. It has made the transition from a print to a digital product with no hitches. This is a good way to update your research since it indexes journals 4 to 6 weeks before they are picked up by ILP and LRI. It is available on LexisNexis, Westlaw and the web.

14.　http://web5s. silverplatter.com/webspirs/ start.ws.

10.4   Law-related Journal Indexes

At some point a legal researchers may need to
search for journal articles from other disciplines,
like political science, public policy, or economics.
Some of the best indexes to search for articles from
these areas include EconLit,[15] Worldwide Political
Science Abstracts,[16] and PAIS International.[17]
There are also many full-text databases in other
areas that are useful for researching legal topics.
These include Contemporary Women's Issues,[18]
GenderWatch,[19] and Ethnic NewsWatch.[20] For example, if you are researching property rights of
women in Africa, you should search the legal literature as well as PAIS International, Contemporary
Women's Issues, and GenderWatch. Searching these
databases retrieves many articles on the rights of
married women in Africa from journals that would
not be covered in the legal journal indexes. These
databases are often available at an academic library.
Asking a reference librarian for help in finding the
right index and for assistance in how to use it is a
good idea.

Of course, there are some freely available web
tools for locating journal literature. While none of

15.   http://www.econlit.org/
accesslist.html.

16.   http://www.csa.com/
factsheets/polsci-set-c.php.

17.   http://www.csa.com/
factsheets/pais-set-c.php.

18.   http://www.oclc.org/
support/documentation/

firstsearch/databases/
dbdetails/details/CWI.htm.

19.   http://www.il.proquest.
com/products_pq/descriptions/
genderwatch.shtml.

20.   http://www.il.proquest.
com/products_pq/descriptions/
ethnic_newswatch.shtml.

these provide the depth of access found in the databases listed above, they can be useful for legal research on a budget. The University of Texas Law School Library hosts Contents Pages from Law Reviews and Other Scholarly Journals, a searchable database of tables of contents from more than 750 law reviews and other scholarly publications related to the law published in the United States and abroad.[21] Another is Washington & Lee Law School's Current Law Journal Content, which covcrs ovcr 1330 law journals.[22] For example, a search of the Washington & Lee site for articles on "international arbitration" produces many citations to recent literature (see Figure 1). You can also see the entire table of contents for selected journals (see Figure 2).

21. http://tarlton.law. utexas.edu/tallons/content_ search.html.

22. http://lawlib.wlu.edu/ CLJC/index.aspx.

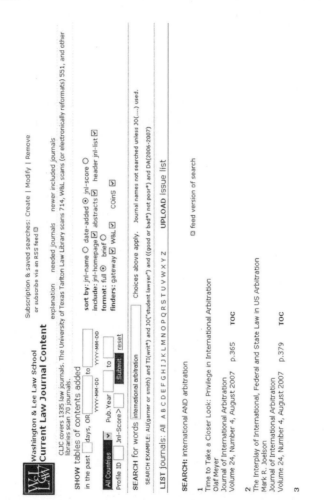

Figure 1: Results Page from W & L Database

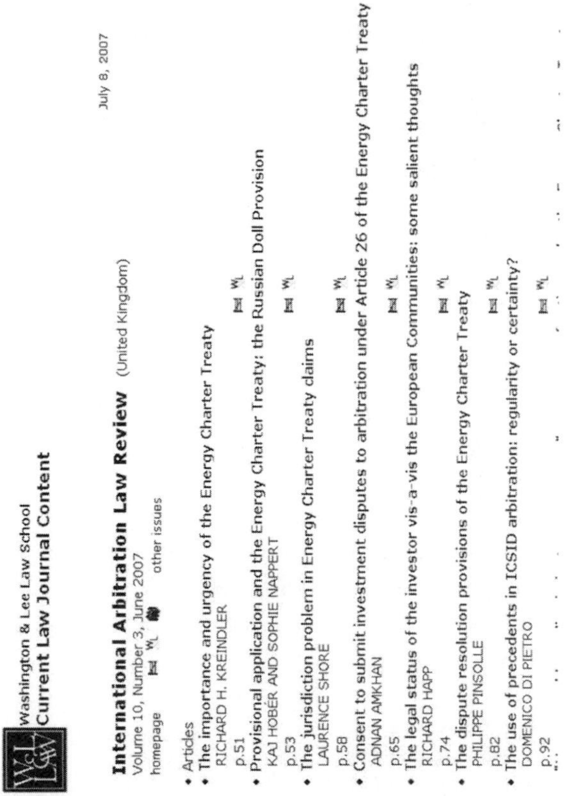

Washington & Lee Law School
Current Law Journal Content

July 8, 2007

International Arbitration Law Review (United Kingdom)
Volume 10, Number 3, June 2007
homepage other issues

- Articles
- The importance and urgency of the Energy Charter Treaty
  RICHARD H. KREINDLER
  p.51
- Provisional application and the Energy Charter Treaty: the Russian Doll Provision
  KAJ HOBÉR AND SOPHIE NAPPERT
  p.53
- The jurisdiction problem in Energy Charter Treaty claims
  LAURENCE SHORE
  p.58
- Consent to submit investment disputes to arbitration under Article 26 of the Energy Charter Treaty
  ADNAN AMKHAN
  p.65
- The legal status of the investor vis-a-vis the European Communities: some salient thoughts
  RICHARD HAPP
  p.74
- The dispute resolution provisions of the Energy Charter Treaty
  PHILIPPE PINSOLLE
  p.82
- The use of precedents in ICSID arbitration: regularity or certainty?
  DOMENICO DI PIETRO
  p.92

Figure 2: Table of Content for International Arbitration Review

10.5   Full-text Sources for Journal Articles

LexisNexis, Westlaw and HeinOnline[23] all provide access to the full text of many law reviews and legal journals. None of these databases provide access to every article from every journal, not even all US law reviews but these three come close. Other collections are available for getting the complete text of selected articles from legal journals, including Cambridge University Press,[24] Oxford University Press,[25] JSTOR,[26] and Project Muse.[27]

10.6   Working Papers

Another rich source for commentary and analysis is working and research papers. With the web, scholars are making more and more of these kinds of materials available for free. Traditional legal publishing involves significant delays. By using one of the following series a scholar can have his or her work in circulation quickly, and can issue it as a working paper so that it need not be in final form. Some websites are becoming major repositories of such papers, others provide links to individual working paper series. A few noteworthy ones include:

- Bepress Legal Repository[28]

23.   http://heinonline.org/ HOL/.

24.   http://journals. cambridge.org/.

25.   http://www. oxfordjournals.org/.

26.   http://www.jstor.org/.

27.   http://muse.jhu.edu/.

28.   http://law.bepress.com/ repository/.

- Legal Scholarship Network (LSN)[29]

- Global Law Working Papers[30]

- NELLCO Legal Scholarship Repository[31]

Let's look at LSN a little more closely. LSN is part of the Social Science Research Network (SSRN), which also includes networks for accounting, economics, finance, and information. Assume that you are looking for recent scholarship on "Common article three" of the Geneva Conventions, in light of a recent Executive Order issued by the President. A simple search by title, abstract or keywords on LSN retrieves several useful working papers and new articles (see Figure 3).

29. http://www.ssrn.com/lsn/index.html.

30. http://www.nyulawglobal.org/workingpapers/glwpsmain.htm.

31. http://lsr.nellco.org/.

☐ **Hamdan and Common Article 3: Did the Supreme Court Get it Right?**
Minnesota Legal Studies Research Paper No. 07-22, Minnesota Law Review, Vol. 91, p. 1525, 2007
Fionnuala D. Ni Aolain.
University of Minnesota Law School
Date Posted: April 23, 2007
Last Revised: May 23, 2007
Accepted Paper Series
68 downloads

☐ **The Collision between Common Article Three and the Central Intelligence Agency**
Catholic University Law Review, Vol. 56, No. 3, 2007, William Mitchell Legal Studies Research Paper No. 85
John Radsan
William Mitchell College of Law
Date Posted: October 18, 2007
Last Revised: October 18, 2007
Accepted Paper Series
4 downloads

☒ **Dutch Courts' Universal Jurisdiction over Violations of Common Article 3 qua War Crimes**
Journal of International Criminal Justice, Vol. 4, Issue 2, pp. 362-371, 2006
Guénaël Mettraux
Affiliation Unknown
Date Posted: July 8, 2006
Last Revised: July 8, 2006
Accepted Paper Series

☐ **The Expressive Value of Prosecuting and Punishing Terrorists: Hamdan, the Geneva Conventions, and International Criminal Law**
Washington & Lee Legal Studies Paper No. 2007-02, George Washington Law Review, Vol. 75, 2007
Mark A. Drumbl
Washington and Lee University School of Law
Date Posted: January 10, 2007
Last Revised: January 10, 2007
Accepted Paper Series
95 downloads

Figure 3: Search results from LSN

There are also many collections of working papers in other disciplines, such as National Bureau of Economic Research (NBER)[32] or the Center for Migration and Development.[33]

32. http://www.nber.org/papers/.

33. http://cmd.princeton.edu/papers.shtml.

There has been much news about Google Scholar[34] and Google Book Search[35] as powerful tools for the researcher. You should remember that these projects are both in beta format and should be used as one of your research tools and not the only one. For now it is best to be careful.

An example makes the point. Suppose I am interested in researching whether there is a human right to water. A search on Google Scholar retrieves some interesting results, such as an article by P.H. Gleick, *The Human Right to Water*, in a journal called *Water Policy* (see Figure 4). It also lists a book by S.M.A. Salman called *A Human Right to Water: Legal and Policy Dimensions*. This search also allows me to take a peek at this book using Google Books. While I cannot view the entire book, I can look at the table of contents and some of the chapters to determine if the book is on point. I can then see if a local library has the book or contemplate purchasing my own copy. To further my research, I can search the three indexes mentioned above–ILP, LRI, and LJI–on Westlaw. A search using the phrase "human rights" and water retrieves many relevant articles. Some of these citations are linked to the full-text of the article on Westlaw and some are not. In fact, an interesting line of articles on this topic was published in the *Netherlands Quarterly of Human Rights*, a title which is not available in full-text on Westlaw. If I

34. http://scholar.google.com/schhp?tab=ps & hl=en.

35. http://books.google.com/bkshp?tab=wp & hl=en.

had relied on just Google Scholar or full-text sources on Westlaw, I would not have discovered this body of commentary. By using both the journal indexes and the Google tools, I now know about many in-depth articles, in both legal and non-legal literature, as well as at least one relevant book. Mixing sources is always wise.

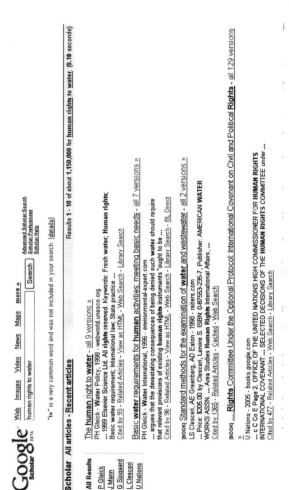

Figure 4: Google Scholar Search

While these two Google projects, and other similar digital collections, seem to offer a lot to the researcher, you need to be aware of the limitations. Without climbing on a soapbox, here are some considerations. One example is the quality of the scanning that is at the heart of the project. It is important to note that the scanned material may not be complete or accurate. A second concern is the completeness of the material's content. Not all of the content from cover to cover is actually freely available; you may only have access to a snippet or a section. The materials available in each project should be searched since there may not be overlap. Each project also has its own way of ranking materials pursuant to a search. As noted earlier, these research aids should be one of the tools you use when trying to locate commentary and analysis. We advise using a library catalog to identify relevant books and then proceeding to search the various digital collections to determine if the book is available on the web, either free or through a subscription service.

This area of international research, like others that we have seen, sometimes lives on the cutting edge of technology and sometimes can only be found in paper form in the stacks of a library. Keep an open mind as you research. Folks who only believe in paper or only live on the internet will lose out.

CHAPTER 11

GENERAL RESEARCH STRATEGIES

11.1   Introduction

If the subject of this Nutshell is International Legal Research, why would there be a chapter about general research strategy? Think of your authors as missionaries who preach a gospel of good research habits. We hope that you have developed solid researching skills from your general experience with legal materials, but at the very least we want to reinforce them. As you gain experience as legal researcher, your skills, habits and methodology will also develop. Working with international legal materials can help you reflect on your more general research habits and patterns. Then there is the view that like green, leafy vegetables and regular exercise, good research skills are just good for you.

An important first step is to recognize that "research" describes a pretty wide range of activity. Sometimes research is a simple act of finding a specific document, like locating a definition or verifying a date. It could be that you want to find a particular treaty or agreement. Other times, research can involve a complex process in which you consult numerous sources and synthesize and analyze what you find. Before doing anything else, decide what it is that you want to do.

Listed below are seven general research strategies (and habits) you should follow no matter what your research project might be. Research is not a linear process and you will not follow each stage and move on to the next. You will constantly be going back and forth between stages during the research process, for some of us that is what makes it fun. It is also why note taking is crucial. Over time, you will develop strategies that work best for you and those strategies will vary depending on the project, the time allowed for the project, and the resources that are available. At that point you will be an expert. Be sure to help those who come asking for assistance.

11.2 The Steps

1. Think Before You Begin Your Research

A little preparation and thought before you jump into a research project can save time and be very valuable, really. Take a few moments to think about your research project. Most human beings want to plunge right into a project; they do not want to think about what they are going to do. They want to go do it. (This must be related to everyone's hatred for reading the directions to their cell phone). But be a good economist. A little time invested at the beginning of your research can save a great deal of time later in the process. Overcome that desire to dive in without a plan and it will pay off.

Consider the following points:

- What are you trying to accomplish or what do you need to research? Try to imagine your ideal answer. What do you want?

- What information do you have before you start? Do you know the relevant law or the relevant facts? Since your research problem is quite likely being generated elsewhere, i.e. handed to you by a professor or a senior lawyer in your organization, get as much information from her as possible. It is amazing how often folks miss the opportunity to explore the parameters of the research query with the person posing it. Be a good interviewer.

- What do you think you need to locate? Is there relevant primary law that you need to locate, such as a treaty or international agreements, national legislation or case law? Do you need to locate factual information such as dates or names? This will determine your direction, it is crucial.

- How much time do you have to spend on this project? This may be dictated by a self-imposed deadline, a paper due date, or how much billable time can be spent on the project. Frequently resources will dictate how much time you can spend and what kind of sources you can use. If you have access to expensive databases you will be doing one kind of research, if you can only use resources freely available on the internet it will be quite different.

Look for a research guide or bibliography on your topic or jurisdiction.

- Locate print and electronic guides and bibliographies. Our research mantra is: find someone who has done the work for you! There are many altruistic souls who have compiled guides and there are many scholars who have exhaustively gathered sources. If someone has done this in your area of interest, find it. Research guides highlight resources and may provide some information regarding research strategy. Traditional bibliographies simply highlight relevant resources.

Keep good notes of what you have done during the course of your research. We do not mean to offend you by repeating advice that may have been provided to you by an elementary school teacher, but good notes are crucial. We shudder at the thought of the legion of folks who have had to retrace their own paths because they forgot where they had gone. It sounds banal but keeping good notes can be efficient and save you time in the end.

- Write down the keywords or terms of art that may be useful. If someone gave you this question to work on she might be a good source. Secondary sources with good indexes can help. Asking a librarian can also work. If you do not know the keywords and the names of important concepts, you can spin your wheels for a long time.

- Make a list of the resources you think you want to consult (specific databases and print resources). Be sure to note the ones you have used and what terms you searched. If something was particularly useful, note that as well. It is also useful to note vagaries in the tools you use, for future reference. This is how you become an expert.

- Prepare a list of the sources as you consult them (like a bibliography). Include the basic bibliographic information (title, publisher, publication date, any information on updates). Be sure to include both print and electronic sources. When including information about an electronic source, include the searches used, the dates searched, and any other relevant information. The date you last viewed the source can be incredibly important.

- Some researchers find checklists to be useful. Some samples are available on the web, see http://www.legalresearch.org/docs/checklist. html or http://lib.law.washington.edu/ref/ statcheck.doc. While these are not geared to international or foreign law, they may be useful as a template.

Don't get side-tracked.

- It is easy to locate something else of interest and spend time in another direction. Stay on point. Unless it is really good.

2. Secondary Sources Are Your Friends

Many researchers think that locating the relevant primary source is the most important first step. Since American law school pedagogy is built around this idea it is not surprising that they do. However, many times you don't know what sources of law are needed or you do not understand the scope of the issues involved. Background or secondary sources can be the best place to start when researching a new issue or unfamiliar area of law because these sources discuss and analyze the law. Sometimes, these sources will even reprint the portions of the primary source that you are after. These sources include books, encyclopedias, journal articles, etc. They are online and in print. Even if a source is not something that you would cite to a court or include

in an article it can still be useful in explaining
background, defining terms and providing citations
to other materials.

Locate and review secondary sources.

- Search for law books and articles on your topic
  using library catalogs, indexes and other databases. Here we are counting on you to have
  some basic research skills. Individual chapters
  in this Nutshell discuss relevant websites, indexes and catalogs. We give you as much specific guidance as possible but you have to be
  willing to make full use of the tools discussed.

- Review what you have gathered and take notes.
  Print out important pages that you find online.
  Photocopy the title page and noteworthy pages
  of paper sources or make note of the bibliographic information and the relevant pages. To
  repeat our refrain, doing this when you first
  encounter the information will save you time
  later.

- Note any citations to international and foreign
  laws, including case law.

- Note other references to other articles, books,
  and other materials and consult these sources
  as well.

3. Primary Sources of Law—The Heart of the Matter

Primary sources are the law–statutes, case law,
regulations, treaties, etc. When researching foreign
and international law, keep in mind that each legal

system is a snowflake—no two are exactly the same. We guide you to sources that will help you find out the sources in each system. Be sure to use them.

Locate the primary sources of law.

- Locate the law cited to in the secondary sources. These sources include treaties, national laws and regulations, and case law.

- Locate an annotated source for legislation, if possible. This may lead you to relevant case law.

- Once you locate one case on point remember that it is a research document itself. It discusses how the relevant judicial body viewed this particular issue at this moment in time. It should contain citations to all relevant documents. It should lead you to other cases, treaties etc.

- If an English language translation is needed, try to locate that as well.

- Once you have some law to start with, look for other related primary sources.

4. Remember That Non-Legal Sources May Be Crucial

- Non-legal information may be needed to develop factual content, such as dates, statistics, and economic or political data. Once again the indexes and secondary source material that will be discussed in the various chapters of this Nutshell will help you out. A good journal article in a non-legal publication might provide invaluable background for you. International law exists in the world of international politics. Consult newspapers and other non-legal sources to get context.

5. Make Sure Your Research Is Up-to-Date

- Is the source that you are citing current? If you are using a database when was it updated? When was your webpage modified?

- If using books be sure to consult pocket parts or supplements, if they are available. American legal researchers are accustomed to very fast and almost seamless updating of materials. International materials may move slowly and be updated at a stately pace. Know the vintage of what you are using.

- Keep in mind that there are not always electronic databases to use for updating laws of other jurisdictions. Indeed, most jurisdictions do not have anything that is equivalent to Shepard's or Keycite. American legal information is by far the most highly developed; do not be deluded into thinking that other countries or international bodies can match it. The internet allows some to do incredible jobs, but the variation in performance is stunning.

6. The Big Question—How Do I Know When I am Done?

- There is no easy answer to this question. It just depends. Go back to the issues outlined when you thought about the project. Have you used all of your time? Is the deadline approaching and it is time to write the paper or file the brief? This is why you need a plan. Do you want to hear sad stories about researchers who waited too long or who did not know when to stop and ended up with nothing when the deadline came upon them? We did not think so. Never forget your allotted time and resources. These usually dictate whether you are done.

• If you start seeing the same sources over and over and you feel you have done a thorough job on the research, you may be done. Many questions do not have answers. If you see the same dilemma over and over, you have probably reached the end. This is the good part, you produce your view on the matter.

7.   Ask for Help

• Ask a reference librarian at your school, institution, law firm or organization, or call someone in an academic law library. Reference librarians live to serve. They want to help you. What may seem the like the world's most complex problem to you might be something that a good reference librarian can solve in seconds (okay, minutes). Use them. At the very least it is helpful to review your project with an information professional to make sure you have covered the basics. Remember, librarians are always on your side.

CHAPTER 12

SOURCE COLLECTING AND
CITE CHECKING

12.1 Introduction

It is a common experience for law students to be asked to collect sources and to cite check citations as a part of working on a journal or serving as a professor's research assistant. This activity is very similar to carrying out normal research in international law, but the product of your efforts will be more focused and tailored to the person who created the assignment. Though research problems are never exactly the same, we thought that it would be useful to provide an overview of how to go about source collecting and cite checking. We will give you some places to start and then six steps to keep in mind as you work. All of the examples in this chapter are from articles that law students had to collect and check. Everything that follows is also helpful in general international legal research as well.

12.2   Some General Sources: Places to Start

When source collecting for a law journal article, you should be aware of the general sources that can help.

- Online catalogs set out a library's holdings and are available on most law library websites. Some folks grow sleepy at the very mention of library catalogs but they are great resources. These library catalogs invariably include handy search tools and helpful aids. They may link you directly to the information or tell you where to find it. Many offer portals to other sites that you might want to search. You should use these catalogs to locate books and journals in your own library. You might find that your library gives you access to the catalogs of other libraries too.

- Consult research guides that are available on the web. These guides cover a variety of topics (treaties, foreign law, human rights, etc.) and are good for late night guidance on locating sources. Remember that finding someone who has done the work for you is the aim of good researchers. If someone has already pulled together sources for you, use it. For example, if you are trying to research the jurisprudence of U.N. human rights bodies, you should check the ASIL Guide to Electronic Resource for International Law: Human Rights.[1] Or, if you need to figure out how to research the law of Burundi, try using the guide called *The Burundi Legal System and Research*, available on the Globalex website.[2]

- Many academic law libraries subscribe to databases that are useful for accessing sources and for checking citations. Databases like the U.N. Treaty Collection, Constitutions of the Countries of the World, and others are enormously helpful. The better a library's budget, the more of these fine tools you will have access to. Ask a reference librarian if you are not sure what your library offers. We have compiled a list of the databases that we find most useful in Appendix A. As ever, things constantly change, so we will try to keep up in our companion website.

12.3 The Six Steps

The following steps outline the process for locating international and foreign legal sources. Keep in

1. http://www.asil.org/ resource/humrts1.htm.

2. http://www. nyulawglobal.org/globalex/ Burundi.htm.

mind that this is general guidance and may not work for every source. In this section, we will assume that you are source collecting and cite-checking an article.

1. Review the Sources

Review all of the sources you need to collect and break them down into categories: primary sources and secondary sources. Check the text of the article when a citation is unclear.

Primary sources include:

- Treaties and international agreements
- Foreign law (statutes and caselaw)
- International caselaw
- Documents from intergovernmental organizations (such as U.N., EU, or WTO)

Secondary sources include:

- Books
- Articles (law and law-related)
- Newspaper articles
- Reports
- Documents from nongovernmental organizations
- Other (working papers, conference proceedings, etc.)

For more information on primary and secondary sources in international and foreign law, see Chapter 1 of this Nutshell.

2. Decipher the Abbreviations used in Citations

Translate the abbreviations used in the article by using the sources listed below. If none of these tools work, ask your friendly librarian for assistance. It is best to translate them all before you start.

- *Bieber's Dictionary of Legal Abbreviations* (5th ed. 2001). The 4th ed. is available on LexisNexis.

- *The Bluebook: A Uniform Style of Citations* (18th ed. 2005). In particular, see the Tables.

- *Noble's International Guide to the Law Reports* (2002). Good for case reporters for many different jurisdictions.

- *World Dictionary of Legal Abbreviations* (1991–). Arranged by language (German, Spanish, etc.) and by subject.

- Cardiff Index to Legal Abbreviations.[3]

  Covers many international and foreign legal sources.

3. http://www.legalabbrevs.cardiff.ac.uk/

- *Guide to Foreign and International Legal Citations* (2006).[4] Provides lots of information for citing and abbreviating foreign and international legal sources.

4.   http://www.law.nyu.edu/ journals/jilp/gfilc.html.

Figure 1: Cardiff Website

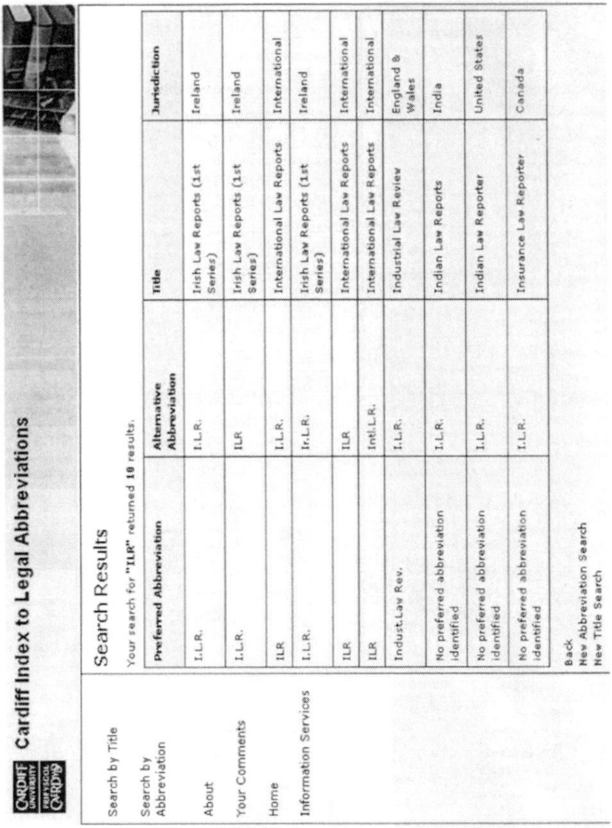

Cardiff Index to Legal Abbreviations

Search by Title

Search by Abbreviation

About

Your Comments

Home

Information Services

Search Results

Your search for **"ILR"** returned 10 results.

Preferred Abbreviation	Alternative Abbreviation	Title	Jurisdiction
I.L.R.	I.L.R.	Irish Law Reports (1st Series)	Ireland
I.L.R.	ILR	Irish Law Reports (1st Series)	Ireland
ILR	I.L.R.	International Law Reports	International
I.L.R.	Ir.L.R.	Irish Law Reports (1st Series)	Ireland
ILR	ILR	International Law Reports	International
ILR	Intl.L.R.	International Law Reports	International
Indust.Law Rev.	I.L.R.	Industrial Law Review	England & Wales
No preferred abbreviation identified	I.L.R.	Indian Law Reports	India
No preferred abbreviation identified	I.L.R.	Indian Law Reporter	United States
No preferred abbreviation identified	I.L.R.	Insurance Law Reporter	Canada

Back
New Abbreviation Search
New Title Search

Figure 2: Example from Cardiff Website

II.   CITATION GUIDE

Citation is quite uniform although there are neither binding rules regarding citation nor a national citation manual in Germany.

0.1 Common Abbreviations

Common abbreviations in German citation practice include Article ("§", "Artikel" or "Art."), paragraph ("Absatz" or "Abs."), and clause ("Satz" or "S."). The "Abs." and "S." symbols are optional (*i.e.*, "Art. 1 Abs. 1 S. 1" = "Art 1 I 1").

Figure 3: Sample Entry from *Guide to Foreign and International Legal Citations*

3. Locate the International Legal Sources Contained Within the Article

Treaties and Agreements

In Step 2, you translated your citations and you find that you need a treaty. One way to get the document is to go directly to the cited source.

If you need a citation to a treaty or international agreement, try searching EISIL[5] or consult Frequently–Cited Treaties and Other International Instruments[6] (this site also includes a quick list of abbreviations and sources for treaties). Otherwise, consult some of the following databases to help you locate the correct citation:

- U.N. Treaty Collection (a database containing treaties deposited with the Secretary General and those published in the *United Nations Treaty Series*)[7]

- U.S. Treaties and International Agreements (if the U.S. is a party) (subscription database)[8]

- LexisNexis and Westlaw

Example 1:

Your citation reads:

Agreement on Trade–Related Aspects of Intellectual Property Rights, Apr. 15, 1994, Marrakesh Agreement Establishing the World Trade Organization, Annex 1C, The Results of the Uruguay Round of Multilateral Trade Negotiations: The Legal Texts 365, *reprinted in* 33 ILM 81 (1994) [herein after TRIPs Agreement].

5. http://www.eisil.org.

6. http://www.law.umn. edu/library/tools/pathfinders/ most-cited.html.

7. http://untreaty.un.org/ English/access.asp.

8. http://www.oceanalaw. com/.

Take a look at Frequently–Cited Treaties and Other International Instruments. From this website, the citation is provided in proper format with a link to the text of the agreement.

Agreement on Trade–Related Aspects of Intellectual Property Rights, Apr. 15, 1994, Marrakesh Agreement Establishing the World Trade Organization, Annex 1C, 1869 U.N.T.S. 299; 33 I.L.M. 1197 (1994).

International Trade and Economic Law

Note: The US did not adopt the 1994 WTO/Marrakesh agreements as treaties; thus, there is no US citation for these documents.

Agreement on Agriculture, Apr. 15, 1994, Marrakesh Agreement Establishing the World Trade Organization, Annex 1A, 1867 U.N.T.S. 410 [no I.L.M. citation]

Agreement on Trade-Related Aspects of Intellectual Property Rights, Apr. 15, 1994, Marrakesh Agreement Establishing the World Trade Organization, Annex 1C, 1869 U.N.T.S. 299; 33 I.L.M. 1197 (1994)

Final Act Embodying the Results of the Uruguay Round of Multilateral Trade Negotiations, Apr. 15, 1994, 1867 U.N.T.S. 14; 33 I.L.M. 1143 (1994)

General Agreement on Tariffs and Trade, Oct. 30, 1947, 55 U.N.T.S. 194; 61 Stat. pt. 5; T.I.A.S. No. 1700

General Agreement on Tariffs and Trade 1994, Apr. 15, 1994, Marrakesh Agreement Establishing the World Trade Organization, Annex 1A, 1867 U.N.T.S. 187; 33 I.L.M. 1153 (1994)

General Agreement on Trade in Services, Apr. 15, 1994, Marrakesh Agreement Establishing the World Trade Organization, Annex 1B, 1869 U.N.T.S. 183; 33 I.L.M. 1167 (1994)

Figure 4: Section from Frequently Cited Treaties Site

Example 2:

Your citation reads:

See Vienna Convention on the Law of Treaties, 23 May 1969 [Vienna Convention], U.N. Doc. A/CONF. 39/27, art. 30, 1155 U.N.T.S. at 339–40.

Use EISIL[9] to confirm cite; use print version of U.N.T.S. or U.N. Treaty Collection for text of this treaty.

For more assistance locating the text of treaties, see Chapter 4 of this Nutshell.

U.N. Documents

If you have a U.N. document number (cited as "U.N. Doc."), try locating the document by using the following websites:

- Official Document Service (ODS)[10]

  Official U.N. documents from 1993; also provides access to the resolutions of the General Assembly, Security Council, Economic and Social Council and the Trusteeship Council from 1946 onwards. Documents are available in PDF.

- UNBISnet[11]

  Search by keywords and U.N. document numbers; coverage is from 1979 onwards. Some full-text documents are available.

- U.N. Documentation Centre[12]

  A good source for U.N. resolutions and other selected documents.

Example 1:

9. http://www.eisil.org.

10. http://documents.un.org/.

11. http://unbisnet.un.org/.

12. http://www.un.org/documents/.

Your citation reads:

UN General Assembly Resolution ES–10/14, *Illegal Israel actions in Occupied East Jerusalem and the rest of the Occupied Palestinian Territory.*

ES–10/14 means Emergency Special Session, 10th session, 14th resolution. The document, in PDF, is available from the U.N. Documentation Centre.[13]

If you have no idea what ES–10/14 means, try searching "ES–10/14 general assembly resolution" on Google. Many of the first results provide links to the text of the resolution. The U.N. Documentation Centre provides you with pretty much all resolutions.

Example 2:

Your citation reads:

Preliminary Analysis: The Humanitarian Implications of the February 2005 Projected West Bank Barrier Route, United Nations Office for the Coordination of Humanitarian Affairs.

A fast way to approach this one is to do a Google search: "Preliminary Analysis: The Humanitarian Implications of the February 2005 Projected West Bank Barrier Route" "United Nations Office for the Coordination of Humanitarian Affairs". This search locates a PDF version of this document from a NGO website.[14]

Example 3:

Your citation reads:

SC Res. 452 (July 20, 1979).

13. http://www.un.org/ga/documents/liemsps.htm.

14. http://www.humanita rianinfo.org/opt/docs/UN/OCHA/BarrierProjections_Feb05_En.pdf.

Search any one of the U.N. websites noted above (ODS, U.N. website, UNBISnet) to obtain a copy of the desired Security Council resolution.

For more assistance with locating U.N. documents, see Chapter 8.

European Union Materials

If you have citations for EU (EC or EEC) documents, try the following sites:

- EUR–Lex[15]

  EU Law Portal which provides access to the *Official Journal* (OJ), COM documents, and more.

- COM documents[16]

  Commission's database; can search by number or keyword.

- European Court of Justice[17]

Example 1:

Your citation reads:

Markets in Financial Instruments Directive of April 21 2004, 2004/39/EC, 2004 O.J. (L145/1).

Search the *Official Journal (OJ)* using the EUR–Lex website. Many of the more recent issues of the OJ are available in PDF.

15. http://eur-lex.europa.eu/en/index.htm.

16. http://ec.europa.eu/transparency/regdoc/recherche.cfm?CL=en.

17. http://curia.europa.eu/en/.

Example 2:

> Your citation reads:
>
> European Parliament and of the Council on Financial Collateral Arrangements of March 27 2001, COM(2001)168 final.
>
> Search the COM documents database noted above.

For more assistance with researching the EU, see Chapter 7.

WTO Documents

Use Documents Online[18] on the WTO website; generally no print version exists. Many GATT documents are also available from the WTO website.[19] Panel reports are commonly referred to in articles (cited as WT/DS), here are some good sources:

- Dispute settlement section of the WTO website.[20] Can search by document number.

- Worldtradelaw.net[21] is a good source for panel reports and other related documents.

Example 1:

> Your citation reads:
>
> United States—Import Prohibition of Certain Shrimp and Shrimp Products, Appellate Body Report, WT/DS58/AB/R.
>
> This is a WTO panel report, see WTO website or worldtradelaw.net; locate by date, country or topic.

---

18. http://docsonline.wto.org/gen_home.asp?language=1. & _=1.

19. http://www.wto.org/english/docs_e/gattdocs_e.htm.

20. http://www.wto.org/english/tratop_e/dispu_e/dispu_e.htm.

21. http://www.worldtradelaw.net/ (subscription database).

For more assistance with WTO documents and materials, see Chapter 9.

International Case law

If you have a citation, decipher the abbreviation and go directly to the source by searching a library catalog by the title of the source. Otherwise, try the website of the international court or tribunal.

To locate the website of the court or tribunal, try EISIL or WorldLII's International Courts & Tribunals Project.[22]

Example 1:

Your citation reads:

Emilio Augustin Maffezini v Kingdom of Spain, ICSID Case NOARB/97/7, JAN.25 2000, 16 ICSID Review—Foreign Investment Law Journal 212 (2001).

Search a library catalog by the title of the journal—*ICSID Review*.

Example 2:

Your citation reads:

Case 26/62, Van Gend & Loos v. Nederlandse Administratie der Belastigen, 1963 ECR 1.

Figure out the abbreviation; ECR is *European Court Reports* (from the European Court of Justice), available in print and from the Court's website.[23]

4. Locate Foreign Legal Sources (Non-U.S. Materials)

Use Foreign Law Guide[24] for information about

22. http://www.worldlii.org/int/cases.

23. http://curia.europa.eu/en/.

24. http://www.foreignlaw.guide.com/ (subscription database).

the jurisdiction and sources. The *Guide to Foreign and International Legal Citations* (2006)[25] can help with foreign abbreviations. See also the *Bluebook* for help with information on selected jurisdictions, see Table 2.

Constitutions and Statutory Law

Example 1:

Your citation reads:

Constitution of South Africa, Chapter 2, § 39(1).

Most constitutions can be found in a set called *Constitutions of the Countries of the World* (both print and electronic).[26]

Example 2:

Your citation reads:

Human Rights Act, 1988, c. 42 (Eng.), in 7 Halsbury's Statutes of England and Wales 528 (4th ed. 2001).

In this case, search a library catalog for *Halsbury's Statutes of England and Wales*. If no source is cited, consult the Foreign Law Guide database for ideas on where statutes are published for specific jurisdictions.

National Case law

Example 1:

Your citation reads:

Ireland K(C) v K(J), [2004] 1 ILR 224.

Decipher abbreviation and get the title of the reporter. Search a library catalog by the name of the publication—*International Law Reports*.

---

25. http://www.law.nyu. edu/journals/jilp/gflic.html.

26. http://www.oceanalaw. com/default.asp (subscription database).

Example 2:

Your citation reads:

In re Ning Yi–Ching, 56 T. L. R. 3 (Vacation Ct. 1939).

Decipher abbreviation, look up title of reporter. Search a library catalog by the name of the publication—*Times Law Reports*.

Example 3:

Your citation reads:

Decision of French Cour de Cassation, *reprinted in* XXIV I.L.O.M. 360 (1984).

There is no such source as I.L.O.M.; the citation should be 24 I.L.M. 360 (1985). Do not spend hours trying to figure out abbreviations—ask a librarian.

Some national case law may be available on the web or in journal literature. Keep in mind that case law can be difficult to obtain and may not be available in English.

For further assistance with researching non-US law, see Chapter 3.

5. Locate Books and Journal Articles

Search for books and journals by using library catalogs or Firstsearch (a database of libraries around the globe, good for determining if a title exists and which library owns it).[27]

Search by author or title first and then try keyword searching. In most catalogs, keyword searches include author names, editor names, and words from the title. Sometimes citations in articles are incorrect, so always check the title by doing a

27. http://firstsearch.oclc. org (subscription database, but many academic libraries subscribe to it).

keyword search. Be sure to drop the initial article when searching by title.

Book Chapters

Example 1:

Your citation reads:

Don Greig, *"International Community", "Interdependence" and All That ... Rhetorical Correctness?, in* State, Sovereignty, and International Governance 521, 530–31, 566 (Gerard Kreijin et al. eds., 2002).

Look up the title of the book on a library catalog (*State, Sovereignty, and International Governance*). The clue here is the word *in*—usually, you cannot look up the chapter, you must look up the title of the book.

Books

Example 1:

Your citation reads:

PH Fouchard et al., *Traite de l'Arbitrage Commercial International* (1996).

Look up the author or the title on a library catalog.

Example 2:

Your citation reads:

Nye, Joseph S., *Bound to Lead: The Changing Nature of American Power,* New York: Basic Books, 1990.

You can search a library catalog by author of title.

Tip: as more books become available on the web, you may have luck locating the book or the chapter through some of these collections, such as Google Books, Project Guttenberg, or the Internet Public Library. Some libraries subscribe to electronic book collections too.

Legal Journals

Sometimes you will need to verify a citation because the citation information is incomplete, incorrect or you need to decipher an abbreviation. Use one of the journal indexes to get accurate information, see Chapter 10 for more information:

- Index to Legal Periodicals and Books (ILP)
- Legal Resource Index (LRI)
- Index to Foreign Legal Periodicals (IFLP)
- Legal Journals Index (LJI)

Example 1:

Your citation reads:

Benedict Kingsbury, *The Tuna–Dolphin Controversy, the World Trade Organization and the Liberal Project to Reconceptualize International Law*, 5 Y.B. Envt'l L. 1, 10 (1994).

Search a library catalog for the title of the publication—*Yearbook of International Environmental Law*.

Example 2:

Your citation reads:

Pierre Legrand, *Civil Law Codification in Quebec: A Case of Decivilianization*, 1 Zeitschrift für Europäisches Privatrecht 575 (1993).

Search a library catalog for the title of this German periodical—*Zeitschrift für Europäisches Privatrecht*.

6. Copying

It's good practice to copy the title page or jot down the name and date of the source on the copy.

12.4 Electronic Sources

Electronic sources are acceptable if no print source is available. Be sure to use the best (most authoritative) electronic version possible. Transcripts and press conferences generally do not have print equivalents.

12.5 Some Cite-checking Tips

Since the *Bluebook* is not always adequate for citing international and foreign legal materials, use the examples in the *Bluebook* as models. Be sure to include enough information so that someone else can find the cited materials. And, be consistent throughout the entire document. For help with proper abbreviations and formats, see the tables at the back of the *Bluebook*.

When you cannot find any guidance in the *Bluebook*, look at other examples from other top law reviews.

When citing to an electronic version of a document, be sure to follow rule 18 of the *Bluebook*.

Finally, when stymied or confused, ask for help. As stated throughout this Nutshell, that's why librarians are there.

CHAPTER 13

STAYING AHEAD OF
THE CURVE

13.1 Introduction

Now that you have made it to the end of this Nutshell, one crucial question remains. How do you stay on top of new resources? You know that even as you read this sentence someone is creating a new webpage that is relevant to your topic? And how can you possibly keep track of new legal developments? Not to worry, we will clue you in to a few tools and a bit of technology that will allow you to monitor websites and stay up-to-date on current information.

13.2   New Developments

These tools are good for keeping track of new developments and topics within international law. Every field develops a set of publications that are read by everyone who works in the area. Most of these sources do not have the depth of a journal article, but they benefit from being frequent and current. If everyone who matters is reading them, then you will be a part of the cutting edge of what is going on. Skimming these can make you look smart.

ASIL Insights
http://www.asil.org/insights.htm
Brief outlines and analysis of new developments or significant events in international law. You can subscribe via email or RSS feed. This is a fine way to keep yourself on top of new developments.

International Law in Brief
http://www.asil.org/ilib/ilibarch.htm
An electronic alert about new developments in international law, such as new treaties or cases. This one you subscribe to via email.

International Judicial Monitor
http://www.judicialmonitor.org/current/index.html
"An international resource for judiciaries, justice sector professionals, and the rule of law community around the world." We discussed this one earlier, it can be a big help. You can subscribe via a RSS feed.

Harvard International Law Journal Digest
http://www.harvardilj.org/digest/
Provides information on legal news and events
from around the world. You can subscribe to
email summaries. The summaries are enough to
put you on alert. Besides, it has the name Harvard attached to it.

International Enforcement Law Reporter (1985–)
http://www.ielr.com/
A monthly newsletter that tracks and summa-
rizes key developments in international law and
related areas. Topic areas generally include money laundering, drug trafficking, taxation, extradi-
tion, asset forfeiture, human rights, cybercrime
and intellectual property.

International Law Update (1995–)
"A monthly report on international legal develop-
ments affecting the United States." Available on
LexisNexis.

Global Legal Monitor (GLM)
http://www.loc.gov/law/public/glm/index.htm
An electronic publication of the Law Library of
Congress that is intended for those who have an
interest in legal developments from around the
world. The Law Library of Congress is a tremendous resource. It employs legal specialists from all
over the globe and it is responsible to Congress.
But you pay the salaries of the specialists, so use
them.

13.3 Blogs

Blogs have also become an important tool for learning about new legal developments. Blogs provide even more up-to-date coverage than the sources mentioned above. Some blogs provide analysis and commentary and some report on new issues and ideas. The quality ranges from the ridiculous to the sublime. Here are some general international law blogs:

Opinio Juris
http://opiniojuris.org/
"A weblog dedicated to reports, commentary, and debate on current developments and scholarship in the fields of international law and politics."

IntLawGrrls
http://intlawgrrls.blogspot.com/index.html
"[V]oices on international law, policy, practice." The felicitous title cues you in that you may find some provocative thinking on this one.

Exploring International Law
http://explore.georgetown.edu/blogs/?blogID=2

International Law
http://blogs.law.harvard.edu/internationallaw/

International Law Reporter
http://ilreports.blogspot.com/

International Law Observer
http://internationallawobserver.eu/

Transnational Law Blog
http://transnationallawblog.typepad.com/
transnational_law_blog/

Comparative Law Blog
http://comparativelawblog.blogspot.com/

Of course, as with everything else, there are topic-specific blogs too, such as:

Human Rights Bloggers
http://www.humanrightstools.org/bloggers.htm

International Economic Law and Policy Blog
http://worldtradelaw.typepad.com/ielpblog

Forced Migration Current Awareness Blog
http://fm-cab.blogspot.com/

Grotian Moment: The International War Crimes Trial Blog
http://law.case.edu/centers/cox/grotian_moment/

The watering hole at which all blogs can be found is Blawg–"Your Source for Legal Blogs, Podcasts & News Feeds."[1] Other useful legal blogs often cover international legal topics. These include:

Legal History
http://legalhistoryblog.blogspot.com/

The Jurisdynamics Network
http://www.jurisdynamics.net/

Law Professors Blogs
http://www.lawprofessorblogs.com/

To learn about new sources and documents, check out these blogs:

DocuTicker
http://www.docuticker.com/

1. http://www.blawg.com/.

"A daily update of new reports from government agencies, ngo's, think tanks, and other groups."

The Gov Docs Guy
http://govdocsblog.kentlaw.edu/wordpress/

inter alia
http://www.inter-alia.net/index.php
A legal research blog.

U.N. Pulse: Connecting to U.N. Information
http://unhq-appspub–01.un.org/lib/dhlrefweblog.nsf
Alerts readers to recent U.N. news and publications.

Opinio Juris

A weblog dedicated to reports, commentary, and debate on current developments and scholarship in the fields of international law and politics

UN and IOs | International Courts and Tribunals | International Law in US Cts | IL Theory and Teaching
US Diplomacy and National Security | International Security | Human Rights | Trade, Economics, and Environment

Contributors

Chris Borgen
Website
SSRN

Peggy McGuinness
Website
SSRN

Julian Ku
Website
SSRN

Roger Alford
Website
SSRN

Kevin Jon Heller
Website
SSRN

Duncan Hollis
Website
SSRN

Peter Spiro
Website
SSRN

Wednesday, December 12, 2007

Kosovo's Status: The Intra-EU Debate, the Role of "Law Talk," and Next Steps
by Chris Borgen

The past few days has seen an intense internal EU debate over the stance the EU should take concerning the status of Kosovo. It is interesting to see how talk about international law was deployed as a tool of statecraft. As discussed in my last post, Russia has had a turn toward "legalization" as it became clear that the political process was not going their way. Here I'll look at the EU internal debate.

Chinese news agency Xinhua reports (emphasis added):

> *Romanian Defense Minister Teodor Melescanu said [in Belgrade] on Tuesday that his country's parliament would not recognize the unilateral declaration of the independence of Kosovo.*

> *"A unilateral decision could have a very negative effect on the entire region and is **not in keeping with international law**," Melescanu told a joint press conference with his Serbian counterpart Dragan Sutanovac.*

Romania has an interest in supporting Serbia: it has had good diplomatic relations with Serbia and, on top of that, Romania would not want to inadvertently support any claim for secession by the ethnic Hungarian population in Romanian Transylvania. For them, then, reference to international legal norms disfavoring secession has been part of their diplomatic stance on Kosovo.

Romania was not the only EU country with concerns. The Xinhua report continues:

> *Commenting different views among the EU members on the future status of Kosovo, Melescanu said that Romania would try to have its stand prevail.*

Figure 1: Opinio Juris Blog

Go

A service of the United Nations
Dag Hammarskjold Library

Connecting to UN information

About

About UN Pulse
Comments/Questions

Recent Entries

Medicine for Children
UNCTAD Review of Maritime
Progress for Children
Follow-up to the Outcome
Renewable Energy
Human Rights Day
Our stories
UNDP Annual Report 2007
New NGO Website
System-wide ethics

December 11th, 2007

Medicine for Children

Posted at 1:01:52 PM in Specialized Agencies | | Permanent Link: Medicine for Children

The World Health Organization (WHO) has launched a new initiative to promote the development of medication for children, **Make Medicine Child Size**. According to the WHO, many medicines are not developed for children or available in suitable dosages or formats; and when they are they are not reaching the children who need them most. Learn 10 Facts, the campaign targets, or check out the list of essential medicines for children (full text, pdf, 362 KB).

December 11th, 2007

Figure 2: UN Pulse

13.4 RSS Feeds

RSS (Really Simple Syndication, Rich Site Services) is a syndication tool that allows you to read current postings from websites and blogs, without needing to visit each individual web source. If you are not too familiar with RSS feeds, watch this video: RSS in Plain English.[2] It should tell you all that you need to know. For a list of law-related RSS feeds, see RSS Feeds for Legal Topics.[3] Many blogs and websites noted in this chapter provide feeds.

2. http://www. commoncraft.com/rss_plain_english.

3. http://www.virtualchase. com/topics/law_rss_feeds.shtml

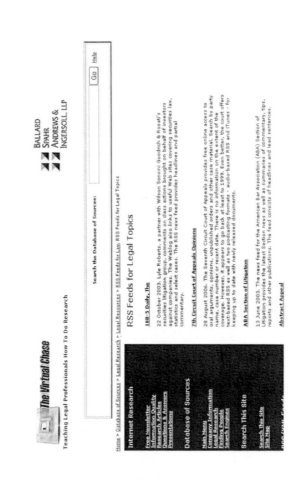

Figure 3: RSS Feeds

13.5 Podcasts

As anyone who has not been living in Justice Souter's world knows, podcasts are available on many topics. This is a short list of where to find some international and foreign law related podcasts, but there are many more available.

University of Chicago Law School
Contains some international law related podcasts.
http://uchicagolaw.typepad.com/faculty/podcasts/index.html

Georgetown University Law School
Contains some international law related podcasts.
https://www.law.georgetown.edu/webcast/

Human Rights Watch Podcasts
http://www.hrw.org/doc/?t=podcasts

Yale Law School Podcasts
http://cs.law.yale.edu/blogs/podcasts/archive/tags/international + law/default.aspx

And, finally, check out our companion website for more new stuff in the future.

http://www.law.berkeley.edu/library/intlnutshell/.

*

APPENDIX A
COMPREHENSIVE SOURCE LIST

This is a comprehensive list of the sources cited throughout this Nutshell, including print sources, subscription databases, and freely available websites. For updated links and sources, see http://www.law.berkeley.edu/library/intlnutshell/. We will endeavor to keep this site up-to-date.

For access to subscription databases, check with a friendly reference librarian at your law library.

AFRICAN YEARBOOK OF INTERNATIONAL LAW (1994–), also available on HeinOnline, http://heinonline.org (subscription database).

Duncan Alford, European Union Legal Materials: An Infrequent User's Guide, http://www.nyulawglobal.org/globalex/European_Union.htm.

American Society of International Law, Guide to Electronic Sources for International Law, http://www.asil.org/resource/home.htm.

American University Washington College of Law, Basic Documents and Jurisprudence of International Criminal Courts and Tribunals, https://www.wcl.american.edu/warcrimes/wcro_docs/.

Amnesty International, http://web.amnesty.org/library/engindex.

An Annotated Guide to Web Sites around the World (Harvard Law Library), http://www.law.harvard.edu/library/services/research/guides/international/web_resources/.

Maureen Ratynski Andersen, *Where to Begin . . . When You Don't Know How to Start: Tips for Researching U.N. Legal Materials*, 31 INT'L J. LEGAL INFO. 264 (2003).

John G. Apple and Robert P. Deyling, *A Primer on the Civil–Law System,* http://www.fjc.gov/public/pdf.nsf/lookup/CivilLaw.pdf/$file/CivilLaw.pdf.

ASIL Insignts, http://www.asil.org/insights.htm.

AustLII, http://www.austlii.edu.au/au/cases/cth/HCA/.

Australian Department of Foreign Affairs and Trade, http://www.dfat.gov.au/.

Australian Treaties Library, http://www.austlii.edu.au/au/other/dfat/.

Australian Treaty Series, http://www.austlii.edu.au/au/other/dfat/treaties/.

AUSTRALIAN YEARBOOK OF INTERNATIONAL LAW (1966–), also available on HeinOnline, http://heinonline.org (subscription database).

Auswartiges Amt, http://www.auswaertiges-amt.de/diplo/de/Startseite.html.

Babel Fish, http://babelfish.altavista.com.

bepress Legal Repository, http://law.bepress.com/repository/.

ROBERT C. BERRING ET AL., HOW TO FIND THE LAW (9th ed. 1989).

Blawg, http://www.blawg.com/.

BNA'S EASTERN EUROPE REPORTER (1991–).

BOLESLAW A. BOCZEK, INTERNATIONAL LAW: A DICTIONARY (2005).

IAN BROWNLIE, PRINCIPLES OF PUBLIC INTERNATIONAL LAW (6th ed. 2003).

THOMAS BUERGENTHAL & SEAN D. MURPHY, PUBLIC INTERNATIONAL LAW IN A NUTSHELL (4th ed. 2007).

BULLETIN ON CONSTITUTIONAL CASE-LAW (1993–), also available online via Codices Database, http://www.venice.coe.int/site/main/CODICES_E.asp.

William E. Butler, RUSSIAN LAW (2nd ed. 2003).

Cambridge Journals Online, http://journals.cambridge.org/ (subscription database).

Canada, Acts of Parliament, http://canadagazette.gc.ca/partIII/index-e.html.

Cardiff Index to Legal Abbreviations, http://www.legalabbrevs.cardiff.ac.uk/.

CCH CONGRESSIONAL INDEX (1938–).

Center for Migration and Development, http://cmd.princeton.edu/papers.shtml.

CHARTER OF THE UNITED NATIONS: A COMMENTARY (Bruno Simma ed., 2nd ed. 2002).

China Laws for Foreign Business, http://business. cch.com/ipnetwork (subscription database).

Collection of Laws for Electronic Access (CLEA), http://www.wipo.int/clea/en/index.jsp.

COMMERCIAL LAWS OF EUROPE (1978–).

COMMERCIAL LAWS OF THE WORLD (dates vary), also available online via RIA Worldwide Tax Law, http://checkpoint.riag.com/ (subscription database).

Comparative Law Blog, http://comparative lawblog.blogspot.com/.

COMPARATIVE LAW IN THE 21ST CENTURY (Andrew Harding & Esin Örücü eds., 2002).

BENEDETTO CONFORTI, THE LAW AND PRACTICE OF THE UNITED NATIONS (3rd rev. ed. 2005).

Constitution Finder (University of Richmond Law School), http://confinder.richmond.edu/.

CONSTITUTIONAL JURISPRUDENCE OF THE FEDERAL REPUBLIC OF GERMANY (2nd ed. 1997).

CONSTITUTIONS OF THE COUNTRIES OF THE WORLD (Albert P. Blaustein & Gisbert H. Flanz eds., 1971–), also available online by subscription, http://www.oceanalaw.com.

Contemporary Women's Issues, http://www.oclc. org/support/documentation/firstsearch/databases/ dbdetails/details/CWI.htm (subscription database).

Contents Pages from Law Reviews and Other Scholarly Journals (University of Texas School of

Law Library), http://tarlton.law.utexas.edu/tallons/content_search.html.

Council of Europe, Treaty Office, http://conventions.coe.int/.

Council of the European Union, http://www.consilium.europa.eu/showPage.ASP?lang=en.

Current Law Journal Content (Washington & Lee Law School), http://lawlib.wlu.edu/CLJC/index.aspx.

CURRENT TREATY INDEX (Igor I. Kavass & Adolf Sprudzs, eds., 1991–), available on HeinOnline, http://www.heinonline.org/ (subscription database).

CURIA (European Court of Justice), http://curia.europa.eu/en/transitpage.htm.

CUSTOMARY INTERNATIONAL HUMANITARIAN LAW (2005).

CUSTOMARY INTERNATIONAL LAW ON THE USE OF FORCE: A METHODOLOGICAL APPROACH (2005).

HENRY SAINT DAHL, DAHL'S LAW DICTIONARY: FRENCH TO ENGLISH/ENGLISH TO FRENCH: AN ANNOTATED LEGAL DICTIONARY, INCLUDING DEFINITIONS FROM CODES, CASE LAW, STATUTES, AND LEGAL WRITING =DICTIONNAIRE JURIDIQUE DAHL (2nd ed. 2001), also available on LexisNexis.

HENRY SAINT DAHL, DAHL'S LAW DICTIONARY: SPANISH–ENGLISH/ENGLISH–SPANISH: AN ANNOTATED LEGAL DICTIONARY, INCLUDING AUTHORITATIVE DEFINITIONS FROM CODES, CASE LAW, STATUTES, AND LEGAL WRITING

=DICCIONARIO JURIDICO DAHL (4th ed. 2006), also available on LexisNexis.

PETER DE CRUZ, COMPARATIVE LAW IN A CHANGING WORLD (3rd ed. 2005).

DIGEST OF COMMERCIAL LAWS OF THE WORLD (N. Stephan Kinsella & Paul E. Comeaux, eds., 1998–).

DIGEST OF UNITED STATES PRACTICE IN INTERNATIONAL LAW (1973–1980, 2001–), documents available at Digest of International Law, http://www.state.gov/s/l/c8183.htm.

DocuTicker, http://www.docuticker.com/.

DOING BUSINESS IN ARGENTINA (1998–).

DOING BUSINESS IN ASIA (1991–).

DOING BUSINESS IN MEXICO (1980–).

Early English Books Online, http://eebo.chadwyck.com/home (subscription database).

EAST EUROPEAN CASE REPORTER OF CONSTITUTIONAL LAW (1994–).

Ebrary, http://www.ebrary.com/corp/libraries.jsp (subscription database).

EconLit, http://www.econlit.org/accesslist.html (subscription database).

Electronic Information System for International Law (EISIL), http://www.eisil.org.

Electronic Journal of Comparative Law, http://www.ejcl.org/.

ELGAR ENCYCLOPEDIA OF COMPARATIVE LAW (Jan M. Smits ed., 2006).

International Organizations: Nongovernmental Organizations Research/Subject Guide (Emory Libraries), http://web.library.emory.edu/subjects/socsci/polsci/igongo.html.

ENCYCLOPEDIA OF ASSOCIATIONS: INTERNATIONAL ORGANIZATIONS (1989–), also available electronically at http://galenet.galegroup.com (subscription database).

ENCYCLOPEDIA OF EUROPEAN UNION LAW (1996–).

ENCYCLOPEDIA OF PUBLIC INTERNATIONAL LAW (1981–1990, 1992–).

Ethnic Newswatch, http://www.il.proquest.com/products_pq/descriptions/ethnic_newswatch.shtml (subscription database).

EU Institutions and Other Bodies, http://europa.eu/institutions/index_en.htm.

Eur–Lex, http://europa.eu.int/eur-lex/lex/en/index.htm.

EUROPA DIRECTORY OF INTERNATIONAL ORGANIZATIONS (1999–), also available electronically at http://www.europaworld.com (subscription database).

Europa (EU Portal), http://europa.eu/.

European Court of Auditors, http://eca.europa.eu/portal/page/portal/eca_main_pages/home.

European Court of Human Rights, http://cmiskp. echr.coe.int/tkp197/default.htm.

European Court of Justice, http://curia.europa.eu/ en/transitpage.htm.

European Economic and Social Committee, http:// eesc.europa.eu/index_en.asp.

European Journal of Legal Studies, http://www. ejls.eu/index.php?.

European Union, Council of the European Union (Council of Ministers), http://www.consilium. europa.eu/.

European Union, European Commission, http:// ec.europa.eu/index_en.htm.

European Union, European Parliament, http:// www.europarl.europa.eu/news/public/default_en. htm?redirection.

European Union: A to Z Index, http://www. eurunion.org/infores/euindex.htm.

Exploring International Law, http://explore. georgetown.edu/blogs/?blogID=2.

Extraordinary Chambers in the Courts of Cambodia, http://www.eccc.gov.kh/english/default.aspx.

Finlex, http://www.finlex.fi/en/.

FirstSearch, http://firstsearch.oclc.org (subscription database).

First Ten Years of the Korean Constitutional Court: 1988–1998 (2001).

Ralph Folsom, European Union Law in a Nutshell (5th ed. 2005).

Forced Migration Current Awareness Blog, http://fm-cab.blogspot.com/.

Foreign and Commonwealth Office, http://www.fco.gov.uk/.

Foreign and International Law Resources: An Annotated Guide to Web Sites Around the World, http://www.law.harvard.edu/library/services/research/guides/international/web_resources/treaties.php.

Foreign Law Guide, http://www.foreignlawguide.com/ (subscription database). The print version is called THOMAS H. REYNOLDS & ARTURO A. FLORES, FOREIGN LAW: CURRENT SOURCES OF CODES AND BASIC LEGISLATION IN JURISDICTIONS OF THE WORLD (1989–). The print will be discontinued in favor of the electronic.

NIGEL FOSTER, GERMAN LEGAL SYSTEM & LAWS (3rd ed. 2002).

JAMES FOX, DICTIONARY OF INTERNATIONAL AND COMPARATIVE LAW (3rd ed. 2003).

Frequently–Cited Treaties and Other International Instruments (University of Minnesota Law Library), http://www.law.umn.edu/library/tools/pathfinders/most-cited.html.

GenderWatch, http://www.il.proquest.com/products_pq/descriptions/genderwatch.shtml (subscription database).

General Agreement on Tariffs and Trade (GATT) Digital Library, http://gatt.stanford.edu/page/home.

Georgetown University Law School, https://www.law.georgetown.edu/webcast/.

CLAIRE GERMAIN, GERMAIN'S TRANSNATIONAL LAW RESEARCH (1991–),the French chapter is available at http://library2.lawschool.cornell.edu/encyclopedia/countries/france/default.htm.

Germain's International Court of Justice Research Guide (Cornell University Law Library), http://library.lawschool.cornell.edu/WhatWeDo/ResearchGuides/ICJ.cfm.

German Law Archive, http://www.iuscomp.org/gla/.

German Law Journal, http://www.germanlaw journal.com/index.php.

H. PATRICK GLEN, LEGAL TRADITIONS OF THE WORLD (3rd ed. 2007).

MARY ANN GLENDON, COMPARATIVE LEGAL TRADITIONS IN A CHANGING WORLD (2nd ed. 1999).

Globalex, http://www.nyulawglobal.org/globalex/index.html.

Global Legal Monitor, http://www.loc.gov/law/public/glm/index.htm.

L.M. GOODRICH ET AL., CHARTER OF THE UNITED NATIONS: COMMENTARY AND DOCUMENTS (3rd ed. 1969).

Google Book Search, http://books.google.com.

Google Scholar, http://scholar.google.com/

The Gov Docs Guy, http://govdocsblog.kentlaw. edu/wordpress/.

Government Gazettes Online, http://www.lib. umich.edu/govdocs/gazettes/index.htm.

Grotian Moment: The International War Crimes Trial Blog, http://law.case.edu/centers/cox/ grotian_moment/.

GUIDE TO INTERNATIONAL LEGAL RESEARCH (2002–).

Guide to Foreign and International Legal Citations (2006), http://www.law.nyu.edu/journals/jilp/ gfilc.html.

Guide to Law Online (Law Library of Congress), http://www.loc.gov/law/help/guide.html.

GUIDE TO THE UNITED STATES TREATIES IN FORCE (Igor I. Kavass & Adolf Sprudzs eds., 1982–), available on Heinonline, http://www.heinlinelcom (subscription database).

Hague Conventions on Private International Law, http://hcch.e-vision.nl/index_en.php?act= conventions.listing.

Hague Justice Portal, http://www.haguejustice portal.net/.

Wiltrud Harms, Selected U.N. Resources & Research Tools: Overview and Search Tips for Legal Research, http://www.law.berkeley.edu/library/ online/guides/international_foreign/UNResources ResearchTools.pdf.

TREVOR C. HARTLEY, THE FOUNDATIONS OF EUROPEAN COMMUNITY LAW: AN INTRODUCTION TO THE CONSTITU-

TIONAL AND ADMINISTRATIVE LAW OF THE EUROPEAN COMMUNITY (6th ed. 2007).

Harvard International Law Journal Digest, http://www.harvardilj.org/digest/.

Hauser Global Law School Program, http://www.nyulawglobal.org/workingpapers/glwpsmain.htm.

HeinOnline, Legal Classics: International Law, http://heinonline.org/HOL/Index?index=beal/sub 15 & collection=beal (subscription database).

HeinOnline, Treaties and Agreements Library, http://heinonline.org/HOL/Index?collection= ustreaties & set_as_cursor=clear subscription database.

HEIN'S UNITED STATES TREATIES AND OTHER INTERNATIONAL AGREEMENTS CURRENT SERVICE [microfiche] (1990–), also available on HeinOnline, http://www.heinonline.org (subscription database).

Marci Hoffman, Researching Human Rights Law (Law Library University of California Berkeley), http://www.law.berkeley.edu/library/online/guides/international_51fforeign/humanRights/index.html.

Human Rights Bloggers, http://www.humanrights 51ftools.org/bloggers.htm.

Human Rights Watch, http://hrw.org/reports/2006/icty0706/.

Human Rights Watch Podcasts, http://www.hrw.org/doc/?t=podcasts.

Humanitarian Information Centres and Partners, http://www.humanitarian51finfo.org/opt/docs/UN/OCHA/BarrierProjections_Feb05_En.pdf.

ILO, NATLEX database, http://www.ilo.org/dyn/natlex/natlex_browse.home.

INDEX TO FOREIGN LEGAL PERIODICALS (IFLP) (1960–), also available at http://web5s.silverplatter.com/webspirs/start.ws (subscription database).

INDEX TO LEGAL PERIODICALS AND BOOKS (ILP) (1908–), also available on LexisNexis, Westlaw, and at http://www.hwwilson.com/Databases/legal.htm (subscription database).

Institute for Transnational Law, http://www.utexas.edu/law/academics/centers/transnational/work_new/.

inter alia, http://www.inter-alia.net/index.php.

Inter-American Court of Human Rights, http://www.corteidh.or.cr/.

International Agencies and Information on the Web (University of Michigan), http://www.lib.umich.edu/govdocs/intl.html.

International Centre for Settlement of Investment Disputes, http://www.worldbank.org/icsid/index.html.

INTERNATIONAL COMMERCIAL ARBITRATION IN ASIA (2006–).

International Constitutional Law Project, http://www.servat.unibe.ch/law/icl/index.html.

International Court of Justice, http://www.icj-cij. org/.

International Criminal Court, http://www.icc-cpi. int/home.html.

International Criminal Tribunal for Rwanda, http://69.94.11.53/.

International Criminal Tribunal for the Former Yugoslavia, http://www.un.org/icty/index.html.

International Economic Law and Policy Blog, http://worldtradelaw.typepad.com/ielpblog.

INTERNATIONAL ENCYCLOPAEDIA OF LAWS (dates vary).

INTERNATIONAL ENFORCEMENT LAW REPORTER (1985–), also available online at http://www.ielr.com/.

International Judicial Monitor, http://www. judicialmonitor.org/current/generalprinciples. html.

International Justice Tribune, http://www. justicetribune.com/ (subscription database).

INTERNATIONAL LABOUR LAW REPORTS (1978–), also available on HeinOnline, http://www.heinonline. com (subscription database).

International Law, http://blogs.law.harvard.edu/ internationallaw/.

International Law in Brief, http://www.asil.org/ ilib/ilibarch.htm.

International Law in Domestic Courts, http://ildc. oxfordlawreports.com (subscription database).

International Law Observer, http://international lawobserver.eu/.

International Law Reporter, http://ilreports. blogspot.com/.

INTERNATIONAL LAW UPDATE (1995–), also available on LexisNexis.

INTERNATIONAL LAW REPORTS (1919–).

INTERNATIONAL LAWYER'S DESKBOOK (2nd ed. 2003).

International Legal Research Tutorial, http://www.law.duke.edu/ilrt/.

International Organization for Migration, http://www.imldb.iom.int/.

INTERNATIONAL ORGANIZATIONS (Jan Klabbers ed., 2005).

International Organizations and Related Information (University of Michigan Documents Center), http://www.lib.umich.edu/govdocs/intl.html.

International Organizations Website (Northwestern University), http://www.library.northwestern.edu/govinfo/resource/internat/igo.html.

International Tribunal for the Law of the Sea (ITLOS), http://www.itlos.org/.

IntLawGrrls, http://intlawgrrls.blogspot.com/index.html.

Institute for Transnational Law (University of Texas at Austin Law School), http://www.utexas.edu/law/academics/centers/transnational/work_new/.

Internet Archive, http://www.archive.org/details/millionbooks.

INTRODUCTION TO FOREIGN LEGAL SYSTEMS (1994).

INTRODUCTION TO TURKISH LAW (Tugrul Ansay & Don Wallace, Jr. eds., 5th ed. 2005).

INVESTMENT LAWS OF THE WORLD (1972–).

MARK W. JANIS, AN INTRODUCTION TO INTERNATIONAL LAW (4th ed. 2003).

PHILIP C. JESSUP, TRANSNATIONAL LAW (1956).

JSTOR: The Scholarly Journal Archive, http://www.jstor.org/ (subscription database).

The Jurisdynamics Network, http://www.jurisdynamics.net/.

IGOR KAVASS, WORLD DICTIONARY OF LEGAL ABBREVIATIONS (1991–)

Khmer Rouge Trial Task Force, http://www.cambodia.gov.kh/krt/english/index.htm.

Lawlinks (University of Kent), http://www.kent.ac.uk/lawlinks/eurounion.html.

Law Professors Blogs, http://www.lawprofessorblogs.com/.

LEAGUE OF NATIONS TREATY SERIES (1920–1946), also available through the United Nations Treaty Collection.

Legal History Blog, http://legalhistoryblog.blogspot.com/.

LEGAL JOURNALS INDEX (LJI), no longer available in print, available on Westlaw and through Current

Legal Information, http://www.sweetandmaxwell.co.uk/online/cli.html (subscription database).

LEGAL RESOURCE INDEX (LRI) (1980–), also available at LexisNexis, Westlaw, and as LegalTrac on the web (see next).

LegalTrac, http://www.gale.com/tlist/sb5088.html (subscription database).

Legifrance, http://www.legifrance.gouv.fr/.

Sophie Lobey, History, Role and Activities of the Council of Europe: Facts, Figures and Information Sources, http://www.nyulawglobal.org/globalex/Council_of_Europe.htm.

LLRX.com, http://www.llrx.com/category/1050.

PETER MALANCZUK, AKEHURST'S MODERN INTRODUCTION TO INTERNATIONAL LAW (8th rev. ed. 2002).

Making of Modern Law, http://www.gale.com/ModernLaw/ (subscription database).

MARTINDALE-HUBBELL INTERNATIONAL LAW DIGEST (1993–2006). The print version was replaced with a CD–Rom and is also available on LexisNexis.

P.S.R.F. MATHIJSEN, A GUIDE TO EUROPEAN UNION LAW (9th ed. 2007).

Max Planck Institute for Comparative Public Law and International Law, http://www.mpil.de/ww/en/pub/research/details/publications/institute/prax.cfm.

MAX PLANCK YEARBOOK OF UNITED NATIONS LAW (1998–).

Kent McKeever, Researching Public International Law (Columbia University Law Library), http://www.law.columbia.edu/library/Research_Guides/internat_law/pubint.

WERNER MENSKI, COMPARATIVE LAW IN A GLOBAL CONTEXT: THE LEGAL SYSTEMS OF ASIA AND AFRICA (2nd ed. 2006).

Migration Law Database (International Organization for Migration), http://www.imldb.iom.int/.

Million Book Project, http://www.archive.org/details/millionbooks.

MODERN LEGAL SYSTEMS CYCLOPEDIA (1984–).

MULTILATERAL TREATIES DEPOSITED WITH THE SECRETARY GENERAL (1982–), also available as part of UN Treaty Collection database.

MyILibrary, http://www.myilibrary.com/ (subscription database).

NAFTA Claims, http://www.naftaclaims.com/.

NAFTA Secretariat, http://www.nafta-sec-alena.org/DefaultSite/index_e.aspx?DetailID=5.

National Bureau of Economic Research (NBER), http://www.nber.org/papers/.

Nations of the World (Library of Congress), http://www.loc.gov/law/guide/nations.html.

NELLCO Legal Scholarship Repository, http://lsr.nellco.org/.

AccessUN, http://infoweb.newsbank.com (subscription database).

NGO Research Guide (Duke University Libraries), http://docs.lib.duke.edu/igo/guides/ngo/.

NOBLE'S INTERNATIONAL GUIDE TO THE LAW REPORTS (2002).

OCLC, http://www.oclc.org/home.

Office of High Commissioner for Human Rights (OHCHR), http://www.ohchr.org/english/law/index.htm.

Official Document System (ODS), http://documents.un.org/.

Open Content Alliance, http://www.opencontentaliance.org/.

Opinio Juris, http://opiniojuris.org/.

L. OPPENHEIM, OPPENHEIM'S INTERNATIONAL LAW (Robert Jennings & Arthur Watts, eds., 9th ed. 1992).

Organization for Economic Co-operation and Development (OECD), http://www.oecd.org/.

Organization for the Prohibition of Chemical Weapons, http://www.opcw.org/.

EDMUND JAN OSMANCZYK, THE ENCYCLOPEDIA OF THE UNITED NATIONS AND INTERNATIONAL AGREEMENTS (3rd ed. 2003).

OXFORD HANDBOOK OF COMPARATIVE LAW (Mathias Reimann & Reinhard Zimmermann eds., 2006).

Oxford's International Law in Domestic Courts, http://ildc.oxfordlawreports.com (subscription database).

Oxford Journals, http://www.oxfordjournals.org/ (subscription database).

PAIS INTERNATIONAL, http://www.csa.com/ factsheets/pais-set-c.php (subscription database).

PARRY AND GRANT ENCYCLOPAEDIC DICTIONARY OF INTERNATIONAL LAW (John P. Grant and J. Craig Barker eds., 2nd ed. 2004).

Permanent Court of Arbitration, http://www.pca-cpa.org/.

Permanent Court of International Justice, http://www.icjcij.org/pcij/index.php?p1=9.

Jonathan Pratter, À la Recherche des Travaux Préparatoires: An Approach to Researching the Drafting History of International Agreements, http://www.nyulawglobal.org/globalex/Travaux_Preparatoires.htm.

MARY MILES PRINCE, BIEBER'S DICTIONARY OF LEGAL ABBREVIATIONS (5th ed. 2001).

Project Gutenberg, http://www.gutenberg.org/ wiki/Main_Page.

Project MUSE, http://muse.jhu.edu/ (subscription database).

Project on International Courts and Tribunals, http://www.pict-pcti.org/.

DONALD RAISTRICK, INDEX TO LEGAL CITATIONS AND ABBREVIATIONS (2nd ed. 1993).

Refugee Caselaw (University of Michigan), http://www.refugeecaselaw.org/.

RESTATEMENT OF THE LAW, THIRD, THE FOREIGN RELATIONS LAW OF THE UNITED STATES (1987, annual supplements), also available on LexisNexis and Westlaw.

THOMAS H. REYNOLDS & ARTURO A. FLORES, FOREIGN LAW: CURRENT SOURCES OF CODES AND BASIC LEGISLATION IN JURISDICTIONS OF THE WORLD (1989–). The print will be discontinued in favor of the electronic version, Foreign Law Guide, http://www.foreign lawguide.com/ (subscription database).

RIA Worldwide Tax Law, http://chcckpoint.riag. com (subscription database).

SHABTAI ROSENNE, PRACTICE AND METHODS OF INTERNATIONAL LAW (1984).

RSS Feeds for Legal Topics lists sources of legal contents, http://www.virtualchase.com/topics/law_ rss_feeds.shtml.

RSS in Plain English, http://www.commoncraft. com/rss_plain_english.

RUDDEN AND WYATT'S EU TREATIES AND LEGISLATION (9th ed. 2004).

Silke Sahl, Researching Customary International Law,   http://www.nyulawglobal.org/globalex/ Customary_International_Law.htm.

SELECTED JUDGMENTS OF THE SUPREME COURT OF ISRAEL (1962–).

A Selective List of Guides to Foreign Legal Research (University of Columbia Law Library), http://www.law.columbia.edu/library/Research_ Guides/foreign_law/foreignguide.

SENATE TREATY DOCUMENT SERIES (1981–).

MALCOLM SHAW, INTERNATIONAL LAW (5th ed. 2003).

DINAH L. SHELTON, "Soft Law," *Handbook of International Law* (2008), available at SSRN: http:// ssrn.com/abstract=1003387.

Social Science Research Network (SSRN), http:// www.ssrn.com/lsn/index.html.

Sources of International and Foreign Law in English, http://www.law.uiuc.edu/library/ref_ sources_intl_foreignlaw_english.asp.

Special Court for Sierra Leone, http://www.sc-sl. org/.

STATE PRACTICE REGARDING STATE IMMUNITIES (2006).

TAXATION IN LATIN AMERICA (1987–).

TAX LAWS OF THE WORLD (dates vary), also available online via RIA Worldwide Tax Law, http:// checkpoint.riag.com/ (subscription database).

Thomas: Treaties, http://thomas.loc.gov/home/ treaties/treaties.htm.

Trade Agreements (U.S. Trade Representative), http://www.ustr.gov/Trade_Agreements/Section_ Index.html.

Trade Compliance Center, http://tcc.export.gov/ Trade_Agreements/index.asp.

Transnational Dispute Management, http://www. transnational-dispute-management.com (subscription database).

Transnational Law Blog, http://transnationallaw
blog.typepad.com/transnational_law_blog/.

Treaties and International Agreements Online,
http://www.oceanalaw.com/ (subscription database).

TREATIES AND OTHER INTERNATIONAL AGREEMENTS OF
THE UNITED STATES OF AMERICA, 1776–1949 (1968–
1976).

TREATIES AND OTHER INTERNATIONAL ACTS SERIES
(T.I.A.S.) (1946–).

*Treaties and Other International Agreements: The
Role of the United States Senate: A Study*, prepared for the Committee on Foreign Relations,
United States Senate, S. Print 106–71, (2001),
http://frwebgate.access.gpo.gov/cgi-bin/getdoc.cgi?
dbname=106_cong_senate_print&docid=f:66922.
pdf.

TREATIES IN FORCE (TIF) (1950–), http://www.state.
gov/s/l/treaty/treaties/2007/ index.htm and on
HeinOnline.

Union of International Associations, http://www.
diversitas.org/db/x.php.

U.N. Pulse: Connecting to U.N. Information,
http://unhq-appspub–01.un.org/lib/dhlrefweblog.
nsf.

United Nations, http://www.un.org/.

United Nations Assistance to the Khmer Rouge
Trials, http://www.unakrt-online.org/index.htm.

United Nations Bibliographic Information System (UNBISNET), http://www.un.org/Depts/dhl/unbis net/index.html.

United Nations Documentation Centre, http:// www.un.org/docuuments/.

United Nations Documentation: Research Guide, http://www.un.org/Depts/dhl/resguide/.

United Nations, Economic and Social Council, http://www.un.org/ecosoc/.

United Nations Framework Convention on Climate Change, http://unfccc.int/2860.php.

United Nations, General Assembly, http://www. un.org/ga/.

THE UNITED NATIONS: LAW AND PRACTICE (Franz Cede & Lilly Sucharipa–Behrmann eds., 2001).

United Nations, Secretariat, http://www.un.org/ documents/st.htm.

United Nations, Security Council, http://www.un. org/Docs/sc/.

United Nations, Specialized Agencies and Other Programs, http://www.un.org/aboutun/chart.html.

United Nations Treaty Collection, http://untreaty. un.org/English/access.asp (subscription database).

UNITED NATIONS TREATY SERIES (U.N.T.S.) (1946–), also available online via the United Nations Treaty Collection, http://unaty.un.org/Ensh/access.asp.

United Nations, Trusteeship Council, http://www.
un.org/documents/tc.htm.

United States Bilateral Investment Treaties,
http://www.state.gov/e/eeb/rls/fs/2006/22422.htm.

United States Department of State, http://www.
state.gov/r/pa/ho/frus/.

United States Department of State, Bureau of
International Security and Nonproliferation
(ISN), Treaties and Agreements, http://www.
state.gov/t/isn/trty/.

United State Department of State, Bureau of
Verification, Compliance, and Implementation
(VCI), Treaties and Agreements, http://www.
state.gov/t/vci/trty/.

United States Income Tax Treaties (Internal Revenue Service), http://www.irs.gov/businesses/inter
national/article/0,,id=96739,00.html.

UNITED STATES TREATIES AND OTHER INTERNATIONAL
AGREEMENTS (U.S.T.) (1950–).

UNITED STATES TREATY INDEX (Igor I. Kavass ed.,
1991–).

University of Chicago Law School, http://uchicago
law.typepad.com/faculty/podcasts/index.html

University of Wisconsin Digital Collections, Foreign Relations of the United States, http://digicoll.
library.wisc.edu/FRUS/.

JORGE A. VARGAS, MEXICAN LEGAL DICTIONARY AND
DESK REFERENCE (2003).

GERHARD VON GLAHN & JAMES LARRY TAULBEE, LAW AMONG NATIONS: AN INTRODUCTION TO PUBLIC INTERNATIONAL LAW (8th ed. 2007).

ALAN WATSON, COMPARATIVE LAW: LAW REALITY AND SOCIETY (2007).

WEST'S LAW AND COMMERCIAL DICTIONARY IN FIVE LANGUAGES: DEFINITIONS OF THE LEGAL AND COMMERCIAL TERMS AND PHRASES OF AMERICAN, ENGLISH AND CIVIL LAW JURISDICTIONS (1985).

CHRISTIAN L. WIKTOR, MULTILATERAL TREATY CALENDAR = REPERTOIRE DES TRAITES MULTILATERAUX, 1648–1995 (1998).

WorldCat, http://firstsearch.oclc.org.

Worldcourts.com, http://www.worldcourts.com/pcij/eng/statistics/generalstatistics.htm.

World Law Legal Information Institute, http://www.worldlii.org/.

World Legal Systems, http://www.droitcivil.uottawa.ca/world-legal-systems/eng-monde.html.

WorldLII, http://www.worldlii.org/catalog/2322.html.

Worldtradelaw.net, http://www.worldtradelaw.net/ (subscription database but some content is freely available).

World Trade Organization, http://www.wto.org/.

World Trade Organization, Dispute Settlement Gateway, http://www.wto.org/english/tratop_e/dispu_e/dispu_e.htm.

World Trade Organization Documents, http://www.wto.org/english/docs_e/docs_e.htm.

World Trade Organization, Documents Online, http://docsonline.wto.org/.

Worldwide Political Science Abstracts, http://www.csa.com/factsheets/polsci-set-c.php (subscription database).

WTO and GATT Research (New York University School of Law Library), http://www.law.nyu.edu/library/wtoguide.html.

WYATT AND DASHWOOD'S EUROPEAN UNION LAW (5th ed. 2006).

Yale Law School Podcasts, http://cs.law.yale.edu/blogs/podcasts/archive/tags/international + law/default.aspx.

YEARBOOK OF INTERNATIONAL ORGANIZATIONS (1967–), also available electronically via Union of International Associations, https://www.diversitas.org/db/x.php (subscription database).

YEARBOOK OF THE UNITED NATIONS (1946/47–),

Kong Yuan, *Recent Cases Relating to Arbitration in China*, 2 ASIAN INT'L. ARB. J. 179 (2006).

*

APPENDIX B

WEB TREATY COLLECTIONS

———————

General Collections

EISIL (Electronic System for International Law), http://www.eisil.org

Foreign and International Law Resources: An Annotated Guide to Web Sites Around the World: International Treaties (Harvard Law Library), http://www.law.harvard.edu/library/services/research/guides/international/web_resources/treaties.php

Multilaterals Project, http://www.fletcher.tufts.edu/multilaterals.html

Washlaw Web–Treaties, http://www.washlaw.edu/forint/alpha/t/treaties.htm

Topic-specific Collections or Collections by Issuing Body/Organization

Collections that provide status and ratification information are indicated with an asterisk (*).

Avalon Project (Yale Law School), http://www.yale.edu/lawweb/avalon/avalon.htm

Australian Treaties Library,
http://www.austlii.edu.au/au/other/dfat/

Council of Europe, European Treaties,*
http://conventions.coe.int/

ECOLEX (international environmental law),*
http://www.ecolex.org/index.php

Environmental Law Instruments (UNEP),*
http://www.unep.org/law/Law_instruments/index.
asp

Environmental Treaties and Resource Indicators
(ENTRI),*
http://sedac.ciesin.org/entri/

European Union Treaties,*
http://eur-lex.europa.eu/en/treaties/index.htm
http://eur-lex.europa.eu/en/accords/accords.htm

FAO Treaties (Food and Agricultural Organization),*
http://www.fao.org/Legal/TREATIES/Treaty-e.
htm

Hague Conventions on Private International
Law,*
http://www.hcch.net/index_en.php?act=
conventions.listing

International Civil Aviation Organization (ICAO)
Treaty Collection,*
http://www.icao.int/icao/en/leb/treaty.htm

International Humanitarian Law Database,*
http://www.icrc.org/ihl

ILOLEX (International Labour Organization),*
http://www.ilo.org/ilolex/english/index.htm

IMO Conventions (International Maritime Organization),*
http://www.imo.org/home.asp?topic_id=161

International Fisheries Treaty Database,*
http://www.intfish.net/treaties/index.htm

Juris International,*
http://www.jurisint.org/pub/

Latin American Tax Treaties,
http://www.natlaw.com/treaties/taxtreat.htm

Lex Mercatoria (International Trade/Commercial Monitor),
http://www.jus.uio.no/lm/

NATO Basic Texts,
http://www.nato.int/docu/basics.htm

Organization of American States Treaties,*
http://www.oas.org/juridico/english/treaties.html

Peace Agreements Digital Collection (United States Institute of Peace),
http://www.usip.org/library/pa.html

United Nations Treaty Collection,*
http://www.untreaty.un.org

University of Minnesota Human Rights Library,
http://www1.umn.edu/humanrts/

WIPO Treaties,*
http://www.wipo.int/treaties/index.html

U.S. Treaties and Agreements

Bilateral Agreements (Federal Aviation Administration),
http://www.faa.gov/aircraft/air_cert/international/bilateral_agreements/

Bilateral Agreements, Environment (USAID),
http://www.usaid.gov/our_work/environment/climate/policies_prog/joint_statements.html

Bilateral Investment Treaties and Related Agreements (U.S. State Dept.), http://www.state.gov/e/eeb/ifd/c644.htm

Indian Affairs: Laws and Treaties (Electronic version of the treatise compiled and edited by Charles J. Kappler), http://digital.library.okstate.edu/kappler/

Declassified State Department & Other Agency Documents, International Agreements, http://www.foia.state.gov/SearchColls/CollsSearch.asp.
Note: In June 2007, the State Department removed its collection of international agreements from the Freedom of Information Act Electronic Reading Room page. This collection is now available at http://www.state.gov/m/a/ips/c24150.htm.

International Antitrust and Consumer Protection Cooperation Agreements (FTC), http://www.ftc.gov/oia/agreements.shtm

International Judicial Assistance, Notarial Services, and Authentication of Documents (U.S. State Dept.), http://travel.state.gov/law/info/judicial/judicial_702.html

Income Tax Treaties (IRS),
http://www.irs.gov/businesses/international/
article/0,,id=96739,00.html

Private International Law (U.S. State Dept.),
http://state.gov/s/l/c3452.htm

Trade Agreements (U.S. Department of Agriculture),
http://www.fas.usda.gov/itp/agreements.asp

Treaty Information (U.S. State Dept.),
http://travel.state.gov/law/legal/treaty/treaty_785.html

Trade Agreements (U.S. Trade Representative),
http://www.ustr.gov/Trade_Agreements/Section_Index.html

Trade and Related Agreements (U.S. Department of Commerce),
http://tcc.export.gov/Trade_Agreements/index.asp

U.S. Bureau of Nonproliferation, Treaties, and Agreements,
http://www.state.gov/t/isn/

International Social Security Agreements (U.S. Social Security Administration), http://www.ssa.gov/international/agreements_overview.html

*

APPENDIX C

WEBSITES CONTAINING TRANSLATED NATIONAL LAW

In addition to the sources mentioned in Chapter 3, see the following sites for access to translated national law. See also Foreign Law: Subject Law Collections on the Web for other subject oriented websites.[1]

Subject Collections

Annual Review of Population Law
Covers a variety of topics: abortion, family planning, domestic violence, etc.
http://www.nyulawglobal.org/globalex/Foreign_ Collections.htm

Collection of Laws for Electronic Access (WIPO)
Intellectual property and related laws
http://www.wipo.int/clea/

Collection of National Copyright Laws (UNESCO)
http://portal.unesco.org/culture/en/ev.php-URL_ ID=14076 & URL_DO=DO_TOPIC & URL_ SECTION=201.html

1. http://www.nyulaw global.org/globalex/Foreign_ Collections.htm.

Criminal Law Resources on the Internet (Buffalo Criminal Law Center)
http://wings.buffalo.edu/law/bclc/resource.htm

ECOLEX
National environmental law
http://www.ecolex.org/index.php

Election Law Resource (Ace Project)
http://www.aceproject.org/about-en/index_html

FAOLEX (FAO)
National laws and regulations on food, agriculture, and renewable natural resources
http://faolex.fao.org/faolex/index.htm

Global Competition Forum (IBA)
http://www.globalcompetitionforum.org/

International Center for Non–Profit Law (must register)
http://www.icnl.org/

International Constitutional Law
http://www.servat.unibe.ch/law/icl/index.html

International Digest of Health Legislation (WHO)
http://www.who.int/idhl-rils/frame.cfm?
language=english

Law Reform in Transition States (last updated August 2004)
http://www.cis-legal-reform.org/#legal-database-lexinfosys-eng

Legislationonline.org (OSCE)
Legislation dealing with the rule of law, human

rights and fundamental freedoms
http://www.legislationline.org

Maritme Boundaries Laws (DOALOS)
http://www.un.org/Depts/los/LEGISLATION
ANDTREATIES/

Marriage/Divorce Laws (U.S. Dept. of State)
http://travel.state.gov/law/citizenship/citizenship_
775.html#marriage

Migration Law Database (International Organization for Migration)
http://www.imldb.iom.int/.

NATLEX (ILO)
Labor law, social security
http://www.ilo.org/dyn/natlex/natlex_browse.home

REFWORLD (UNHCR)
Law relating to refugees, asylum seekers, state-
less persons
http://www.unhcr.org/cgi-bin/texis/vtx/refworld/
rwmain

UNODC Legal Library
Drug and related legislation
http://www.unodc.org/enl/index.html

U.S. Dept. of State, Bureau of Consular Affairs
The law and policy section contains information
on judicial assistance and more
http://travel.state.gov/law/law_1734.html

VOTA
Electoral database of the Venice Commission
http://www.venice.coe.int/VOTA/en/start.html

World Trade Organization
Good source for laws associated with trade topics, see the trade topics page and the official documents database
http://www.wto.org/

WorldLII: Subjects (a directory of topical web sites)
http://www.worldlii.org/catalog/272.html

Individual Countries/Regions

This is not a comprehensive list, so check out the research guides and other sources noted in Chapter 3. This list contains only freely available sites.

AsianLII
http://www.asianlii.org/

AustLII (Australia)
http://www.austlii.edu.au/

BAILL (UK and Ireland)
http://www.bailii.org/

Cambodia, Laws & Regulations
http://www.moc.gov.kh/laws_regulation/default.htm

CanLII (Canada)
http://www.canlii.org/

CommonLII (The Commonwealth)
http://www.commonlii.org/

Danish Laws in English
http://juraportal.dk/links/010/010/040/?lang=en

Estonian Legislation in English
http://www.legaltext.ee/endefault.htm

Finlex (Finland)
http://www.finlex.fi/en/

Legifrance (France)
http://www.legifrance.gouv.fr/html/codes_traduits/
liste.htm

German Law Archive
http://www.iuscomp.org/gla/archive.htm

HKLII (Hong Kong)
http://www.hklii.org/

Hong Kong, Bilingual Laws Information System
http://www.legislation.gov.hk/eng/home.htm

NZLII (New Zealand)
http://www.nzlii.org/

PacLII (Pacific Islands)
http://www.paclii.org/

Portuguese Legislation in English
http://www.gddc.pt/legislacao-lingua-estrangeira/
english.html

SAFLII (Southern and Eastern Africa)
http://www.saflii.org/

Singapore Statutes Online
http://statutes.agc.gov.sg/

Swedish Statutes in Translation
http://www.sweden.gov.se/sb/d/3288

WorldLII: Countries
http://www.worldlii.org/countries.html

*

INDEX

References are to Pages

---

†